NORWOOD
A HISTORY

THE
MAKING OF AMERICA
SERIES

NORWOOD
A HISTORY

PATRICIA J. FANNING

ARCADIA
PUBLISHING

Copyright © 2002 by Patricia J. Fanning
ISBN 978-0-7385-2404-7

Published by Arcadia Publishing,
Charleston, South Carolina

Printed in the United States of America

Library of Congress control number: 2002109386

For all general information contact Arcadia Publishing at:
Telephone 843-853-2070
Fax 843-853-0044
E-Mail sales@arcadiapublishing.com
For customer service and orders:
Toll-Free 1-888-313-2665

Visit us on the Internet at www.arcadiapublishing.com

FRONT COVER: *The dedication of the Aaron Guild commemorative stone took place during Norwood's 1902 Old-Home Week celebration. The monument still stands on the lawn of the Morrill Memorial Library. (Courtesy Morrill Memorial Library.)*

CONTENTS

ACKNOWLEDGMENTS

In a project of this nature, much of the research depends on the good will of the community involved. Many people shared their stories, some provided archival materials, and others read portions of the manuscript. I am grateful to all for their time, generosity, and knowledge: Curtis and Ethel Balduf, David Benson, Daniel Callahan, Theodore Callahan, Bernard Cooper, Charles Coughlin, Karla Daddieco, Robert Dempsey, Susan Donahue, Helen Abdallah Donohue, Helen Fanning, Margaret Fanning, Rose Riley Fanning, Ronald Frazier, Thomas Furlong, Ellie and Hank Gallant, Irene Gotovitch, Robert W. Hansen, Gloria Head, Aira Koski Johnson, Thomas Judge, Bronius Kudirka, Thomas Lambert, David Lehto, Joan Bonica Lynch, Ellen MacDonald, Roger MacLeod, Henry Maddocks, Elmer Marsh, Ray Martin, Betty Ann McCarthy, Phil McManus, Edmund Mulvehill Jr., Robert Pegurri, Barbara J. Rand, Anne Sansone, Bryant Tolles, Michael Triventi, and Father William Wolkovich.

I extend my appreciation to the Norwood Historical Society's board of governors and the Morrill Memorial Library's board of trustees for access to their respective historical materials and photographic collections.

For their invaluable assistance with portions of my research, I am indebted to the staff of the Morrill Memorial Library, especially Judith Koncz, Marie Lydon, Margot Sullivan, and Director Mary Phinney.

Robert N. Donahue deserves special recognition. His commitment to local history was an inspiration and his enthusiasm and support for this project was greatly appreciated.

My brothers Charles and Geoffrey have been unconditional in their support and encouragement, and have contributed substantially through their own recollections. Finally, I would like to acknowledge my parents, Charles Fanning and Frances P. Balduf Fanning, both life-long Norwood residents. Who I am and how I define my place in the world (and Norwood) are due, in large measure, to them. I have been particularly aware of their influence as this project has progressed and can only hope they would be pleased with the result.

INTRODUCTION

One hundred years ago, in 1902, as Norwood residents dedicated the Aaron Guild commemorative stone, an occasion shown in the photograph on the cover of this book, they were unknowingly on the cusp of a dramatic social and cultural transformation. Justly proud of its heritage, the established community gathered to celebrate its shared past, unaware that, within a decade, immigrants would make up nearly 40 percent of the town's residents. This sudden influx, precipitated by the success of a number of local industries, caught the community off guard. In the accompanying cover photograph of Balch School pupils, *c.* 1910, the children were carefully identified in order as Italian, Irish-American, English, German, Swede, Polish, American, Finn, Syrian, and Lithuanian, a tribute of sorts both to the diversity of the population and the consciousness of difference it had generated.

Within another dozen or so years, in 1922, the town had weathered a housing boom, a world war, and a deadly influenza epidemic, and was about to celebrate its 50th anniversary. Much had changed in that short period of time. Native son F. Holland Day had earned international fame and some notoriety for his advocacy of photography as a fine art and he had amassed a remarkable collection of historical artifacts and documents relating to Norwood. W. Cameron Forbes had built a majestic mansion and intrigued townspeople with his wealth, hobbies, and diplomatic missions. Meanwhile, immigrant groups had become stable, if not prosperous. Inspired by the leadership of George Willett and Frank Allen, the town had undergone municipal restructuring and civic betterment. Aided by Willett's Norwood Civic Association, cultural bridges were being built.

By the middle of the twentieth century, with residents hardened by economic woes and united by yet another war, difference had been replaced by civic commitment. The printing, ink, and tanning industries, which had experienced unprecedented growth in the beginning of the century, had disappeared. The construction of the modern highway system, coupled with post-war prosperity, brought renewed industrial development, municipal reform, and a population explosion. Norwood became a "suburb" and old ethnic identities, once so distinctive, began to recede. As the twentieth century came to a close, three thriving types of business defined Norwood to outsiders: the hospital, the airport, and the Automile. To residents, of course, the community was much more.

Still, the history of the Town of Norwood is captured in the faces of these ten children, looking not simply into the camera, but the future. Norwood was founded by hard-working men and women who labored with their hands to carve a living and a home from the wilderness. It prospered by the labors of the immigrants who took up this same task while toiling in its factories, mills, and tanneries. By the time the town reached its 100th anniversary, its parochial insularity had been breached by highways, commerce, and a more mobile citizenry. Yet, today, in many respects a more prosperous and sophisticated place, Norwood continues to be a community with small town values. Family, community, and country remain paramount as officials, residents, neighbors, and friends together try to balance the town's proud heritage with its modern growth potential.

These ten Balch School pupils from around 1910 were identified by name and nationality. From left to right are (front row) Mary Sansone and Mary Dowdie; (second row) Selina Howarth, Edna Schaier, Allan Carlson, and John Esolitis; and (third row) Sumner Bagley, Bruno Maki, Ed Lewis, and Annie Okonovich. (Courtesy Morrill Memorial Library.)

1. From Settlement to Independence

The Town of Norwood, along with 14 other communities in eastern Massachusetts, began life as part of Dedham. The huge land grant awarded by the General Court in 1636 to the proprietors of Dedham, originally called Contentment, extended from what is now Wellesley and Natick to Bellingham, Wrentham, Plainville, and the Rhode Island border. Prior to this grant, it is believed the original title was acquired by Governor John Winthrop from Algonquin sachem Chickataubet, a transaction confirmed at the request of colonists by Chickataubet's grandson Josias Wampatuck around 1685. There had been no permanent Native American settlements within Norwood's current borders, but its meadows and marshlands were inhabited by an abundance of animals and birds, and its network of brooks feeding into the Neponset River were well stocked with fish and turtles. An archaeological dig, conducted in the early 1980s, prior to the development of land along the Neponset River, unearthed artifacts that lent credence to the legend that the area was used as a hunting ground by nomadic tribes.

As the population of Dedham increased, the outermost settlements began to form their own independent towns. These secessions were precipitated by the then existing General Court laws that required residents to pay taxes in support of Dedham's Church of Christ, whether or not they were voting members of the church community. In addition, all town residents were required to attend church services. As might be imagined, such restrictions and obligations became a hardship on settlers who were building their homesteads miles from the village center. Inhabitants began requesting of the court the right to build and support their own meetinghouses, freeing members from the arduous journey to, and financial support of, the Dedham church. By the first quarter of the eighteenth century, several towns had been established and new centers of settlement continued to emerge.

Although transient colonists occasionally located within the boundaries of present-day Norwood as early as the 1650s, it is generally agreed that the first permanent settler was Ezra Morse, a third-generation descendant of a Dedham

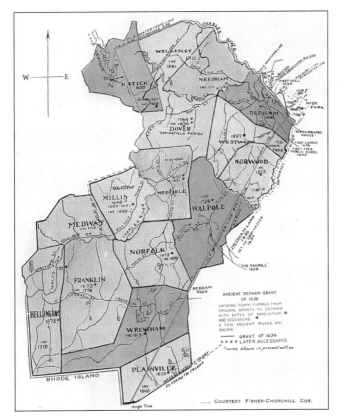

The Town of Norwood, Massachusetts was originally part of the land grant awarded to the proprietors of Dedham in 1636. The grant and subsequent town divisions are shown in this map. (Courtesy Dedham Historical Society.)

resident. Offered land in largely uninhabited South Dedham primarily because of ongoing disputes over water rights with other mill operators and Dedham farmers, gristmill owner Morse constructed a sawmill beside Hawes Brook in 1678. First using his mill to saw lumber and beams for himself, he built a house, the town's first, in the then traditional saltbox style, on a rise of land that came to be known as Morse Hill. After the mill was relocated from Hawes Brook to the larger Neponset River, the establishment attracted the business of farmers seeking to build homes and a new way of life. By 1699, Morse's son had constructed a combination saw and gristmill on the same site and the family continued to operate a mill at this location, near the East Walpole-Norwood town line, until 1895. The first few settlers, situated for the most part on the fertile land beside the Neponset and along the Traphole and Hawes Brooks, gradually transformed the wilderness into a small, self-contained village that came to be known as Tiot.

The usage and derivation of the word are unclear. Once the nickname for the entire town of Dedham, Tiot had become synonymous with the Hawes Brook area, later South Norwood, by 1765. Pronounced phonetically, "Tie-ot" with the accent on the first syllable, and interchangeably spelled "Tiot" and "Tyot" throughout the town's history, the name was used in common parlance for centuries and today remains a visible symbol of town pride as the name of the high school yearbook. The derivation of the word is equally muddled, but local historians and townspeople generally accept that it refers to native language words signifying "enclosed by waters" or "watering place," a logical assumption since the town is bordered by a river and several smaller streams and brooks. In any event, the small settlement, known alternately as Tiot and South Dedham, continued to attract a hardy population of adventurers, among them Deans, Guilds, Bullards, and Sumners, all familiar names to those who walk the streets of Norwood today.

In the spring of 1717, as the settlement became more stable, the residents of Tiot, like so many other parishioners living considerable distances from the Church of Christ in Dedham, petitioned the town for permission to establish their own place of worship and to cease paying ministerial tax to Christ Church. Although the parish government did not immediately grant the petition, religious services were held as early as 1722 in private homes in South Dedham. Finally, in 1728, Dedham officials agreed to the request and, in 1730, the General Court in Boston sanctioned the establishment of a new parish district, a move that cost the Dedham church considerable membership and tax money. After a dispute between residents of South Dedham and West Dedham (now Westwood) over the location of the new meetinghouse, the court ordered the West Dedham parishioners to return to the Christ Church congregation and those living in Tiot to establish the Second or South Parish. West Dedham became a separate parish two years later.

This oil painting of Morse's mill was completed by Mrs. Mary Tucker Fogg in 1850 when the mill was located on the Neponset River off Washington Street near the East Walpole line. (Courtesy Norwood Historical Society.)

Following this victory, South Dedham villagers erected a meetinghouse centrally located near the spot where the Morrill Memorial Library stands today and, in 1736, the Reverend Thomas Balch of Salem was chosen for the pastorate of the Congregational Church. Working from his gambrel-roofed Georgian-style parsonage, Balch became the religious and social leader of the approximately 78 members of the parish. During the next two decades, South Dedham began to develop an infrastructure separate from its mother town. Nearly 100 years earlier, in 1644, Dedham had established a free public school for boys, which Tiot children no doubt attended, although the distance would make the journey difficult, especially in winter. In 1738, only two years after being given its own church, South Parish villagers requested and were granted a schoolhouse of their own. In 1740, a building was erected in the northern part of South Dedham on land near the site of the Callahan School today. For a time, sessions were brief and itinerant teachers from Dedham staffed the school; but, in 1754, the first schoolmaster hired exclusively for the South Parish school arrived. Four years later, the girls of Tiot were welcomed into the schoolhouse as well.

A further indication of Tiot's growing sense of independence was the establishment of its own cemetery in 1741 on land donated by Ebenezer Woodward. The Parish Burial Ground was carved out of a small tract of hilly

Mrs. Mary Tucker Fogg painted this oil of the Balch parsonage in 1855. Formerly located to the west of the intersection of Washington and Walpole Streets, the building was later demolished. (Courtesy Norwood Historical Society.)

This view of the Siege of Louisburg commemorative stone was taken in the 1930s. Norwood's first bandstand and today's post office can be seen in the background. (Courtesy Morrill Memorial Library.)

terrain at the northern end of the village and served as the final resting place of residents until the Highland Cemetery was founded in 1880. The Old Parish Cemetery, as it is now known, continues to be maintained by the Town of Norwood and, although some families moved their graves and monuments to the Highland Cemetery in the 1890s, the burial ground still contains many eighteenth- and early nineteenth-century grave markers.

Mid-eighteenth century records pertaining to South Parish residents are scarce, making it nearly impossible to reconstruct the daily lives of the villagers in their pioneering community of small-crop farms and mills. There existed no real commercial center in Tiot and isolated settlers were forced to travel the 5 miles to Dedham for any needed supplies and retail goods. South Dedhamites did feel part of the larger community, however, as demonstrated by the participation of some 64 Tiot men in the prolonged Colonial Wars that pit English colonists against the French and their Native American allies. One of the most notable campaigns during this period was the Siege of Louisburg, on the Isle of Cape

13

Breton, in 1745. Among those who took up arms in this effort was Reverend Thomas Balch. Other South Dedham residents traveled to the vicinity of Lake George, New York, to participate in the conflict. Louisburg veterans, including Balch, were memorialized by a stone monument erected and dedicated in 1903 by the Norwood Old-Home Week Association. Of the nine South Parish men who had fought at the great fortress, six lost their lives.

Having returned to parish life, Reverend Balch remained a steadfast leader for decades, even as, in 1769, the growing parish moved from its first meeting place to a new house of worship raised on the west side of the present Lenox Street. At the same time, parishioners also built a second structure, called the Noon House, where the congregation gathered for a noonday meal on Sundays between the lengthy morning and afternoon services. This church annex became a convivial hall for church members, who comfortably shared bread, warmth, and parish gossip. The structure remained on this site until 1874 when it was relocated to Neponset Street; there, it was lost to a fire in 1900.

South Dedham parishioners again answered their nation's call in 1775, this time to take part in the Revolutionary War against Great Britain. As poor, subsistence farmers, few in Tiot had the economic standing to be Loyalists, and as historian Bryant Tolles noted in his history of the town, "support of the American war effort was virtually unanimous." The conflict also brought the parish its first folk hero. Aaron Guild, born in 1728, was a fourth-generation descendant of Dedham proprietor John Guild. A life-long resident of South Dedham, Aaron Guild married three times and had ten children. His homestead stood opposite the First Congregational Church building on Walpole Street, then known as the Wrentham Road. Guild was commissioned into the military in 1758, served in the French and Indian War, was a member of the local Committee of Safety in 1774, and was prepared to serve when called upon the following year. His quick response to the Lexington alarm is described vividly on a commemorative stone, erected during Norwood's Old-Home Week celebration in 1902:

Near this spot
Capt. Aaron Guild
on April 19, 1775
left plow in furrow, oxen standing,
and departing for Lexington,
arrived in time to fire upon
the retreating British.

Also in 1902, following a contest sponsored by the Norwood Business Association, a depiction of the rugged farmer shouldering his rifle and leaving his oxen behind, drawn by George L. Boyden, was selected as the official town seal. The memory of Guild's patriotic deed has been secured in a variety of ways, including the naming of Guild Street, Guild Square, two Guild Schools, and the Guild Medical Building.

Aaron Guild was not the only man from Tiot to take up arms against the British during the years 1775 to 1783, however. Although Dedham never became a battleground itself during the Revolution, more than 100 residents from the South Parish put their lives on the line for the new republic, engaging in military action in the Boston area and as far away as Newport, Rhode Island, and Fort Ticonderoga in New York. At the same time, South Dedhamites who remained at home faced the burden of increased taxation, Continental Army requisitions for food and clothing, an unsteady economy, and fluctuating inflation to ensure victory. As the sounds of war receded and Tiot residents settled back into village life, the future of the rural community was already taking shape.

Situated as it was, South Dedham became an early stop for those traveling between Boston and various Rhode Island destinations. As early as 1729, the Old Roebuck Road, also called the Old Post Road, connecting Boston to Bristol, Rhode Island, passed through the eastern border of Tiot, roughly along modern Pleasant Street. After only a few decades, however, another route, following less difficult terrain and called the Wrentham Road, was opened. By 1767, this highway, passing directly through the center of South Dedham and following Walpole Street toward Wrentham, was home to the first regular stagecoach route between Boston and Providence. Today, it is designated as U.S. Route 1-A. The gradual emergence of the retail and commercial center that the Wrentham Road had fostered, took a tremendous leap forward with the building of the Norfolk

This rendition of Aaron Guild leaving for Lexington on April 19, 1775 has been on the town seal since 1902.

and Bristol Turnpike in 1806. A shorter and more direct route between Boston and Providence, this highway, following the present-day Washington Street, was 24 feet wide and surfaced with gravel and pounded stone. It was constructed by a chartered corporation at a cost of about $5,500 per mile. The founders recouped their investment by positioning toll stations at 10-mile intervals along the road. A summary of the rates, compiled by Norwood historian W.W. Everett, provides a window on the transportation business of the early nineteenth century:

For every coach, phaeton, chariot, or other four-wheeled carriage coach drawn by two horses	25 cents
And if drawn by more than two horses, for each additional horse	4 cents
For every curricle	17 cents
For every cart, wagon, sled, or sleigh drawn by two oxen or horses	10 cents
And if drawn by more than two, for each ox or horse in addition	3 cents
For every chaise, chair, or other carriage drawn by one horse	10 cents
For every sled or sleigh drawn by one horse	6 cents
For every man and horse	4 cents
For all oxen, horses, mules, and neat cattle led or driven besides those in teams and carriages, each	1 cent
For all sheep and swine by the dozen	3 cents

In 1843, the road became a free highway maintained by Norfolk County. The influx of travelers and traffic that the Norfolk and Bristol Turnpike sparked was also an incredible boon to the local economy. For the first time, the gates to wider markets, for both the products of and the consumption by the farmers and small industrialists of the village, were opened.

During the first quarter of the nineteenth century, these transportation breakthroughs had a lasting impact on the small community. The area along the Neponset River, in what is now South Norwood, generally maintained its rural farming and milling operations. Meanwhile, a commercial center emerged farther north at the intersection of the Wrentham Road and the Norfolk and Bristol Turnpike. Known as "The Hook" for the large hitching post where travelers and coach drivers tied their horses, Norwood's first business district gathered around Paul Ellis's tavern, situated at what is now the middle of the town common. Ellis's South Dedham or Tiot Tavern, later called the Norwood House, was an L-shaped edifice built by Ellis and Lewis Rhodes as a country inn around 1797. It held public accommodations, a bar, ballroom, and dining room. Also known variably as South Dedham Hotel and the Norwood Hotel, it was moved to Nahatan Street in 1914 as part of George Willett's downtown municipal improvement plan. The building was eventually demolished to erect more modern commercial structures in the mid-twentieth century.

The Tiot Tavern, later known as the Norwood House and Norwood Hotel, was the headquarters of the International Order of Odd Fellows when this view was taken. It was initially operated by Paul Ellis and Lewis Rhodes in the early 1800s. (Courtesy Hansen and Donahue Collection.)

The village center continued to grow in a haphazard fashion with houses, stores, shops, and stables all situated side by side. For example, Oliver Morse, the village tailor, lived and worked in a saltbox-style house located where St. Catherine's Church now stands. It was remodeled into a tenement and later, was home to the town's first drugstore owned by Francis Tinker. On the southwest corner of Nahatan Street stood the property of Jabez Boyden, where the village's first general store was located. In 1823, the block between today's Cottage and Nahatan Streets, a stone's throw from the Ellis Tavern, housed Guild's Wheelwright Shop and Andrew's Tin Shop. Eventually, in 1843, Fisher Gay bought Boyden's and continued the grocery business there, providing Tiot with space for a post office as well. When the Wheelock Building was erected at Washington and Cottage Streets, Gay moved his enterprise to the new site and was joined there by L.W. Bigelow's dry goods store. By the 1860s, the center of South Dedham was comparatively booming. Jeremiah Hogan's Shoe Store and George Kingbury's clock repair shop on Market Street, and a news dealer, paper emporium, and millinery shop in Village Hall joined existing shopkeepers.

The largest business building in South Dedham, Village Hall, erected in 1860, was a massive wooden Italianate structure with several stores at ground level, and, on the second floor, a hall for community gatherings. It quickly became the heart of the community. In its second-floor rooms, Tiot residents held their parties, dances, church fairs, and even graduation exercises. It was here in 1872 that South Dedham villagers voted to separate officially from their mother town. The building was purchased in 1915 by George F. Willett and moved to

This view of Village Hall was taken after the building was relocated from the Hook to Broadway where it was the home of the Boston Piano Supply Company. (Courtesy Hansen and Donahue Collection.)

the corner of Nahatan Street and Broadway where it stood for decades, home to the Boston Piano Supply Company, the *Norwood Messenger* newspaper, and the Ambrose Press. It burned down in April of 1964, just as the demolition of the landmark had begun.

At the same time South Dedham's central commercial district was developing, an evolution of a different sort was taking place in the small community: the Congregational Church was both expanding and fragmenting. Following the departure of Reverend Balch, the work of the South Parish was continued by its second minister, the Reverend Jabez Chickering. Married to Balch's daughter Hannah, Chickering is perhaps best known today for his house, a fine example of the Federal style, still standing on the corner of Chickering Road and Walpole Street. Chickering led the parish for 36 years until his death in 1812. Having been installed as pastor on July 3, 1776, he had, in hindsight, guided the congregation through the uncertain times between two wars with England. During his tenure, Dedham and South Dedham had transitioned from being part of a British Colony to the Commonwealth of Massachusetts in the United States. Likewise, the government was transformed from a chiefly religious to a secular one.

For most residents, however, the Congregational Church remained at the center of village life and Chickering confirmed the church's secular importance to the community by establishing Tiot's first circulating library. At its inception, it consisted of the pastor's own collection of approximately 95 volumes, stored in an unpretentious, blue pine cabinet. Several parishioners, including Abner, Jacob and Moses Guild, Ebenezer Everett, and George Dean, became subscribing members of the "Social Circulating Library" of South Dedham. For ten years, Chickering loaned books to his subscribers for their edification and enjoyment. When the association dissolved, around 1800, a second, larger organization was created and eventually became the inspiration for a public library later in the nineteenth century. Chickering's original cabinet was sold and is now part of the collection of the Norwood Historical Society.

It was under the Congregational Church's third pastor, the Reverend William Cogswell, that the evolution previously alluded to took place. Ordained in 1815, the Dartmouth College graduate oversaw the building of the congregation's third meetinghouse at the intersection of Washington and Chapel Streets 13 years later. The dedication of "The 1828 Meeting House" as it was popularly referred to, and its adjacent parsonage, also ushered in a new era of crisis for the church. It was at that time that a small group of parishioners chose to leave the South Parish Congregational Church and form a Universalist congregation. Founded in 1793 in Oxford, Massachusetts, Universalism embraced the doctrine of universal salvation, that is, that no matter what the transgression, reconciliation with God was possible for all human beings. In addition, Universalism expanded the notion of individual faith to include social responsibility and strongly advocated for temperance, women's rights, prison reform, and the abolition of slavery. This perspective was in sharp contrast to the then common Calvinistic beliefs in predestination and eternal damnation.

Built in 1806 by Jabez Chickering, the second pastor of the First Congregational Church, the Chickering House still stands on the corner of Walpole Street and Chickering Road. (Courtesy Bryant F. Tolles.)

When the Second Parish of Dedham was formed in 1736, it had been a decision based on geography, not theology; the Congregational Church had remained steadfast in the tenets of Christ Church of Dedham. But now, in 1827, several South Dedham families, mostly young and of a more liberal outlook, stated that they "perceived the falsity of the extreme Calvinistic doctrine" of the Congregationalists and withdrew from the church. Shortly thereafter, they incorporated as the First Universalist Society of South Dedham.

Initially, the Universalists met in the Ellis Tavern, then owned by Joseph Sumner, but in 1829, the group erected and dedicated a meetinghouse of their own on the Washington Street property now occupied by St. Catherine's Rectory. The rift between the two denominations was deep, however, and it took decades for long-standing associations to heal. Despite the suicide of their first pastor, Reverend Alfred Bassett, within the first year of his ministry, the Universalists achieved both respectability and stability by the mid-nineteenth century, helping to turn Tiot into a religiously and socially diverse community.

Another factor providing change within the once bucolic landscape and homogeneous citizenry was the increase of basic manufacturing and industrial operations. Mindful of the fact that settlement had begun with Ezra Morse's sawmill in 1678 on Hawes Brook, South Dedham, from its inception, was attractive to industrial concerns. Old records, maps, and accounts indicate that a variety of mills for the cutting and finishing of wood, the grinding of grain into flour, and the production of cloth were established along the area's waterways during the first few decades of the eighteenth century. Most were short-lived, but sometime around 1776, a man by the name of Abner Guild founded a small tannery at the

This view of the third house of worship of the First Congregational Church, located on Washington Street near Chapel, was taken after its steeple was removed during demolition. The America No. 10 fire station, later called Norwood No. 2, can be seen in the rear. (Courtesy Norwood Historical Society.)

southern end of Tiot on Hawes Brook. Initially used to process the rawhides of local farmers, the tannery flourished. In 1791, John Smith, a seven-year-old boy from a poor family, was apprenticed to Guild, learned the trade, and eventually succeeded him in the arduous enterprise. Smith continued to run the tannery until 1831 when he retired, turning the business over to his son Lyman Smith and his son-in-law George Winslow. The Smith and Winslow partnership was a successful one and each man rose to prominence within the community.

Other early industrial firms included a furniture-making company and a wrapping paper mill. The Willard Everett and Company furniture factory had its start in 1815 when Willard Everett was employed by Jabez Boyden, who had started selling furniture at his general store. In an abandoned gristmill on the Neponset River, Boyden produced furniture, including wooden extension tables, said to be the first ever produced in the area. In 1821, Everett bought Boyden's business and shop, changing its name to Willard Everett and Company. During the 1840s, he moved the growing enterprise to a larger plant on the Norfolk and Bristol Turnpike, currently the site of the Norwood Hospital's Lorusso Building. There the business prospered, employed up to 280 cabinetmakers, and became known as one of the finest manufacturers of furniture in the state. On May 26, 1865, fire destroyed the company's buildings, a not uncommon fate for many of the wooden structures of the nineteenth century. Shortly thereafter, the firm moved to Boston.

In 1832, a factory for the manufacture of wrapping paper was founded by Isaac Ellis and Joseph Day on Hawes Brook at the dam on the east end of Ellis Pond. There is speculation that the dam and Ellis Pond itself was created for this enterprise. Known at the outset as Ellis, Day and Company, the firm passed through several hands and survived fires in 1864 and 1878 before closing permanently after a third blaze in 1886. At its height, the business employed 15 men and shipped more than 170 tons of paper and trunk board annually. Several less ambitious industries also existed for a time in Tiot prior to 1850. A modest factory called C. Ellis Turn Mill manufactured small items such as milk-can stoppers and clothespins next to Purgatory Brook, and Percy Tisdale maintained a sawmill on Bubbling Brook at Pettee's Pond. Robert Thompson processed locally produced hides at his tannery near Hawes Brook, and a blacksmith shop stood on the eastern side of the Old Roebuck Road, today known as Pleasant Street.

With the opening of the Norfolk County Railroad in 1849, what had been a rural, parochial community with a few commercial ventures, two churches, and incipient industry, underwent monumental changes. It seemed wherever the railroad sliced through Tiot, a new or relocated enterprise sprang up. The Winslow and Smith tannery split in 1853 with the Winslow's site enlarging and Lyman Smith and Sons erecting a new facility to the north at Railroad Avenue; Everett's furniture factory moved beside the tracks in 1854. Also that year, Spencer Fuller and Isaac Colburn established the Norwood Iron Foundry. By the 1860s, subsequent to Colburn's departure from the firm and Fuller's

The Willard Everett and Company furniture-making enterprise was located on Washington Street. It was destroyed by fire in 1865. (Courtesy Norwood Historical Society.)

death, the establishment was sold to E.D. Draper and Son. Located on Railroad Avenue, the foundry did a general business as iron founders and machinists, but specialized in castings for light machinery, fine surface work, and japanning. In 1890, the foundry was sold to J.E. Plimpton. Meanwhile, also in 1854, Samuel Morrill set up a small printing shop at the Pleasant Street site formerly occupied by Willard Everett's furniture factory and, by 1856, E. Fisher Talbot had begun the manufacture of printed floor carpets and carriage oil cloths on Hill Street also overlooking the railroad tracks. Such industrial expansion required more workers and resulted in the area's first influx of factory and immigrant laborers, increasing the village's population from a few hundred in 1800 to 1,300 by 1865. This surge in activity inevitably gave rise to a second schoolhouse, new stores, and cottage industries.

During this same time period, two additional Christian denominations put down roots in the community. In 1858, the First Baptist Church was founded. Its initial members, who had previously been part of the West Dedham Baptist Church, consisted of Morses, Bakers, and Boydens, established families in South Dedham. The 44 founding parishioners built their first place of worship, a wooden Italianate structure, in the heart of Tiot's business district, on Washington Street across from today's Vernon Street. Five years later, Roman Catholic residents found a permanent home when the congregation of the Universalist Society, reorganized in 1856 as the Universalist Church, erected a larger building and sold their initial structure to the growing Catholic population. Beginning in the 1840s, Catholics had traveled either to St. Joseph's Church in Roxbury or to the Stone Factory Chapel in South Canton to celebrate Mass. Eventually, the archdiocese, which then encompassed four of the New England states, agreed to offer Mass in South Dedham and services were held three or four times a year at the home of Patrick Fahey. By 1860, visiting priests were offering Mass every second Sunday at various locations, including the Norwood Hotel and Village Hall. In 1862, when the Universalists offered to sell their first house of worship to the Catholic congregation, the proposal was readily accepted. Located at the present site of St. Catherine's Rectory, and dedicated to St. Catherine of Siena on August 3, 1863, the building served the congregation well until the current St. Catherine's was constructed in 1910. Meanwhile, the Universalists moved into an impressive Neo-Georgian sanctuary at the southwest corner of Nahatan and Washington Streets where they remained until 1884 when a tremendous fire destroyed the church, spreading to 13 other buildings and threatening the village center. A short time later, an equally architecturally significant Romanesque Revival building was erected on the same site. It remains standing today as the United Church.

Thus, by the early 1860s, the agricultural village was becoming an industrial center; the rural outpost was emerging as an important railroad and turnpike route; and the once homogeneous religious community had given way to diversity. Still, in 1861, Tiot was once again thrown into turmoil by war. This time, it was the Civil War. As had been the case in 1775, the reaction in South Dedham to the call to arms was immediate and sustained. On April 19,

This first home of the First Baptist Church was dedicated in 1859 and stood on Washington Street across from Vernon Street. It was razed in 1950. (Courtesy Hansen and Donahue Collection.)

1861, one week after the firing on Fort Sumter, the town of Dedham held a meeting at Temperance Hall at which a large number of men volunteered for service immediately. Eventually, over 100 South Parish men marched in several Massachusetts regiments, including the 2nd, 18th, 24th, and 43rd Massachusetts Volunteers and the 35th Massachusetts Regiment, quite a large contingent for a village of only 1,300. This fact did not go unheralded as a patriotic circular of 1862 read in part:

> South Dedham heard the country's call
> With neighboring towns did vie
> And she more than her quota sent
> To conquer or to die.

Many of the men, who trained at the Readville camp east of Dedham Village, carried familiar Tiot names such as Morse, Rhoades, Ellis, and Guild. Remarkably, the South Parish lost only six of its native sons during the conflict. The rest returned home to break free of Dedham and to help establish the town of Norwood.

From the time, in 1730, that the General Court had sanctioned the South Parish, unrest had been smoldering within Tiot village. As South Dedham prospered, building up its commercial center and industrial base, resentment over taxation, public works, and schools increased. Village residents felt they were not receiving adequate resources for their manufacturing growth and were unwilling to underwrite improvements in Dedham that would not raise the quality of life in Tiot. In addition, they continued to be disturbed by inadequate school facilities and the distance they were forced to travel to town meetings. In the years 1870 and 1871, two events took place that finally resulted in the decision by South Dedham residents to petition the Massachusetts General Court for incorporation as a separate town. One involved the school department and the other involved the fire department.

South Dedham residents had had their own elementary school beginning in 1740. This original structure was abandoned in 1788, replaced by two buildings within the Dedham school system: District School No. 6, which stood on what is now Lenox Street, near the end of Cross Street, and District School No. 7, which was built farther south. This latter building, with a Civil War–era mansard-style roof addition, still stands at the northeast corner of Pleasant and Sumner Streets. In December of 1851, the Everett School made School No. 6 obsolete. Named in honor of Israel Everett, a Revolutionary War veteran, the Everett School stood at Guild Square, near the present post office building. This facility, with 1860s additions nearly doubling its size, remained an important educational establishment until it was demolished in 1930. Shortly after the Civil War, in 1867, the first Balch School, named in memory of Reverend Thomas Balch, the South Parish's first pastor, replaced School No. 7. This edifice was itself replaced in 1913 by the second Balch School, still standing today. Within these facilities

Named for a Revolutionary War veteran, the Everett School was erected in 1851. With 1860s-era additions that nearly doubled its size, the school was located near the site of the current post office building. (Picturesque Norwood photo.)

and the small private school founded by Miss Martha May Guild in 1844, the young people of Tiot learned the rudimentary skills any village school could offer. Still, students had to travel to Dedham High School if they wanted to receive any secondary educational instruction, a fact that many village residents resented. In 1870, a committee led by Francis O. Winslow of the Winslow Brothers tannery family, petitioned the town of Dedham for a high school to be located in Tiot. The proposal was voted down at a subsequent town meeting, a vote that spurred the citizens of South Dedham to think seriously about secession.

According to town historian W.W. Everett's research, South Dedham had two fire companies at this time. The first, Washington Number 7, established in 1833, was located near the Hook, on Washington Street on the site of today's St. Catherine's Cushing Hall. America Number 10, located near the end of Walnut Avenue on Washington Street, was intended to watch over the southerly end of town. Neither fire company had sophisticated equipment, depending initially on bucket brigades and, later, on a hand-operated pump on wheels called a "hand tub." These tubs, along with a hose carriage that was nothing more than a large hose-reel on two wheels, were pulled to the site of a fire by the firefighters themselves. Always the center of community camaraderie and social activity, Number 7 had for years celebrated the Fourth of July by ringing the firehouse bell. Just prior to the Fourth in 1871, however, Dedham Selectmen voted to prohibit the practice. When the holiday arrived, fire company steward George E. Metcalf rang the bell in defiance and, in essence, rang in independence for Norwood.

South Dedham's first fire station, Washington No. 7, later renamed Norwood No. 1, was located on Washington Street on the site of St. Catherine's School. A hand-drawn hose wagon and hand tub can be seen in front of the station. (Courtesy Norwood Historical Society.)

Within the year, residents drafted the requisite notice to the Massachusetts secretary of state, informing him that they intended to petition the state legislature to become a separate town. At a meeting held on December 22 in Village Hall, a committee, which included J. Warren Talbot, John C. Park, and Caleb Ellis, was selected to present to the Legislative Committee on Towns an official petition, signed by over 80 percent of the legal voters of the village. This petition requested that a new town be established from land that made up the area then known as the South Parish plus a small portion of Walpole. After initial reservations on the part of Dedham officials were resolved, on February 23, 1872, the act incorporating the Town of Norwood was approved by the General Court and signed by Governor William B. Washburn.

There remains some uncertainty in relation to the naming of the town. It is agreed that on January 23, 1872, the villagers gathered to select an appropriate name for their new community. Several appellations were offered for consideration, including Ames (after Fisher Ames of Dedham), Balch (after Reverend Thomas Balch), Day and Winslow (after well-known businessmen of South Dedham), Lyman, the original suggestion (after Lyman Smith, the popular tannery owner), Hook (after the central business district), and Tiot. After the list was narrowed to eight names, on the second ballot, "Ames" received a majority of the votes. After further discussion, however, on the third ballot, "Norwood" received 65 votes and "Ames" received 59. Subsequently, "Norwood" was declared the unanimous choice.

Disagreement has emerged, however, over exactly who proposed Norwood as a fitting name for the town, and why. In December of 1903, Mrs. Marcia Winslow, a schoolteacher and historian, explained to a Norwood Woman's Club audience that the name had originated with local builder Tyler Thayer, who had found that there was only one other Norwood in the United States. According to Marcia Winslow, Thayer also pointed out that the name "looked well in print, had a pleasing sound, and was easy to write." Nearly 20 years later, however, Francis O. Winslow, quoted in a 1922 newspaper article, stated that the town was named after Henry Ward Beecher's popular novel *Norwood, or Village Life in New England*. Published in 1868, its setting was a typical New England town not unlike South Dedham. According to Winslow, Universalist minister Reverend George Hill had placed the name in nomination. In any event, Norwood was selected and the new town, inhabited by 1,825 residents and encompassing some 10.47 square miles, was officially incorporated.

Municipal independence was greeted on March 6, 1872 by a gala celebration that featured day-long activities, speech-making, and revelry. Those who had taken leadership roles in the territory's separation from Dedham led the "jollification," as it was called. It was no coincidence that many of these forward-thinking men, including George Winslow, George H. Morrill, and Lyman Smith, also were instrumental in the town's subsequent industrial development.

New Town.

The Petitioners and others interested in the formation of a New Town in the South part of Dedham, are invited to meet in

Village Hall.

On Thursday Evening, Jan. 25th,

AT 7 1-2 O'CLOCK.

The NAME and other subjects relating thereto will be considered.

Per order of Committee.

This 1872 broadside called all residents of South Dedham to a meeting to conduct business relating to the formation of their new town. (Courtesy Norwood Historical Society.)

2. INDUSTRIALIZATION AND MODERNIZATION

During the last half of the nineteenth century, as Bryant Tolles noted, "industry completely supplanted agriculture as the economic base of the community." The roots of this transformation had been present from the outset, of course, with the building of Ezra Morse's sawmill in 1678, a business that remained in operation throughout the nineteenth century. Not far from the site of Morse's mill another enterprise, Bird and Son, Inc., had a lasting impact on Norwood as well. One of New England's first paper manufacturers, Bird's actually had its beginning in 1795 in Needham, Massachusetts. There, in a small operation situated on the Charles River, George Bird produced mottled and printing paper. In 1803, Bird relocated his factory to Dedham where he contracted to make bank-note paper for the government until 1812 when he moved yet again to a site on the Neponset River in East Walpole. There, commencing in 1817, the company manufactured three or four kinds of coarse commercial wrapping paper. The business prospered and underwent various organizational and partnership changes during the nineteenth and early twentieth centuries. Under the innovative leadership of Charles Sumner Bird, grandson of the founder, the company began to develop new products, including waterproof wrapping, building, and roofing material. In 1904, Bird constructed a new facility in Norwood, about a mile from his East Walpole site, to house his first roofing mill. Seven years later, a Norwood floor covering factory was opened adjacent to the roofing plant, resulting in a massive manufacturing facility. By the beginning of the twentieth century, Bird and Sons had become a nationwide corporation operating plants across the United States.

Other familiar local business concerns began as part of Bird's, including Hollingsworth and Vose Company, whose founder Zachary Taylor Hollingsworth was a partner in George Bird's early business ventures. In 1871, after Francis W. Bird had taken over management from his father, the two partners divided their property with Bird taking the "Upper Mill" and Hollingsworth the site known as the "Lower Mill" in East Walpole. There Hollingsworth was joined by new partner Charles Vose in 1881. Hollingsworth and Vose became an important employer of workers living in Norwood and helped to keep South Norwood a vital, thriving community within the larger town. Today, with operations in several states and England, the enterprise continues to be a world leader in the industrial battery and filtration business.

The need for machinery at Bird and Son spawned another enterprise that became an important employer of Norwood residents. Bird Machine Company of South Walpole, manufacturer of papermaking machinery and filters, traces its origins to a partnership established by Charles Sumner Bird in the early 1900s. Expanding its patents and producing a broad line of centrifugal, filtration, and thermal equipment, Bird Machine has extended its market to include paper, oil, pharmaceutical, and fine chemical applications. As an independent operating division of Baker Process, the company today has a global reputation as the leader in process equipment application design and engineering. It has a worldwide customer list and a direct operating presence in 19 countries.

In 1776, approximately 100 years after Morse's mill was erected, the tanning and manufacture of raw hides into leather began in the South Parish with Abner Guild's tannery on Hawes Brook, near today's Endicott Street. As previously noted, by 1831, this original business had passed into the hands of Lyman Smith and George Winslow. These brothers-in-law continued as partners until 1853 when the firm was dissolved and each established a distinct family business of his own. George Winslow and his sons Elisha, George, Martin, and Francis continued the tanning of sheep and calfskin at the original location under the name George Winslow and Sons. When the elder Winslow retired in 1860, the business was carried on under the name of Winslow Brothers. Meanwhile, Lyman Smith and

This view of the Endicott Street tannery plant was taken in the early twentieth century after the Winslow Brothers and Lyman Smith's Sons tanneries were consolidated by George Willett. (Courtesy Hansen and Donahue Collection.)

his sons Charles and John built a new tannery beside the railroad tracks at the northern end of town, near the Old Parish Cemetery.

By 1890, both establishments had grown to the point where each employed more than 150 men and were processing over one million hides annually. The Smith tannery, which had changed its name to Lyman Smith's Sons in 1856, when the elder Smith retired, had refined the manufacture of lamb and sheep leather and had grown from a single wooden building to a facility covering more than an acre of prime real estate. By the late 1890s, Winslow Brothers, with the addition of wool pulling and scouring activities, had increased its work force to 275 as its primary products became law book leather, linings for the shoe and boot trades, and sheep leather. George Willett brought about the re-consolidation of the two tanneries in 1901.

One of the town's most innovative businesses was also founded in the nineteenth century. The Norwood Ice Company began in the 1860s when the Ellis family first harvested ice from the Ellis Pond, located off Walpole Street. At the outset, the ice was not marketed widely, but under the direction of Isaac Ellis, the business evolved into a major industry. The success of the operation was aided by West Dedham, now Westwood, dairy farmers who found they needed ice to ensure fresh deliveries. As their businesses grew and their delivery routes widened, the farmers no longer could cut and store a sufficient supply of ice on their own. Within a few years, Ellis had a near monopoly on the ice business in West Dedham and Norwood, with additional routes in Walpole and Roslindale. Business increased steadily as regional consumption rose from 10 to 200 tons per week. Shortly after ownership of the enterprise was transferred from Ellis to

The Railroad Avenue plant of Winslow Brothers and Smith stood on the left side of the railroad tracks. J.E. Plimpton's iron foundry, originally founded in 1854 by Spencer Fuller and Isaac Colburn, was situated on the right side. (Souvenir Album of Norwood.)

This advertisement for the Norwood Ice Company appeared in local business directories for several years during the nineteenth and early twentieth centuries.

NORWOOD ∴ ICE ∴ CO.

ESTABLISHED 1868.

L. D. & E. W. ELLIS, PROPRIETORS,

Successors to ISAAC ELLIS,

— Dealers in —

PURE POND ICE

Supplied in any quanlity desired in Norwood, East Walpole and West Dedham.

WALPOLE STREET, NORWOOD, MASS.

Winslow Brothers and Smith Company in 1909, the operation consisted of five mammoth ice houses.

Cutting and storing the ice was such a fascinating process that the harvesting of the ice crop became family entertainment with people lining the shores of the pond to watch the men at work. The business was, of course, somewhat at the mercy of the weather. An excessive dry spell or a mild winter meant the harvest would be small. Still, remarkably, ice was imported from the north only once in the lifetime of the company; that during the extremely mild winter of 1890. Two of the largest crops were in 1879 and 1905 when the ice was 12 1/2 inches and 15 inches thick respectively. With the advent of manufactured ice, the company at first maintained a separate storage facility to house manufactured product in addition to the pond ice. Once refrigeration systems were perfected, however, the iceman's age had ended and the Norwood Ice Company passed into memory.

Meanwhile, another significant enterprise was increasing the industrial base of the town. In 1856, Samuel Morrill, a printer, publisher, and manufacturer of printing inks, moved his business from Andover, Massachusetts to South Dedham, taking over the small building on Pleasant Street that had previously been occupied by the furniture factory of Willard Everett. Along with his sons George H. and Samuel S. the elder Morrill concentrated on the development of superior printing inks. In 1869, when the original firm was reorganized under the name George H. Morrill and Company, it was already recognized as an important force in the industry. Morrill's grew so fast that, by 1884, the plant had expanded from one small structure to fourteen wooden and brick buildings. In that same year, George H. Morrill Jr. and his brother-in-law Edmund Shattuck joined the firm and, along with George H. Morrill, made the company a worldwide success.

Although the manufacture of colored inks commenced in Norwood in 1905, the company's specialty continued to be perfecting-press ink, which was used in the majority of newspaper offices across the country. With close to 100 employees at the Norwood plant, branch stores and factories were established in Los Angeles, Chicago, New York, Philadelphia, San Francisco, and London, England, with a distributing plant in Toronto, Canada. Modifying its name once again in 1909 to the George H. Morrill Company, the enterprise continued to expand, spreading along a vast expanse of Pleasant Street, near the New York, New Haven & Hartford Railroad station known simply as Morrills. With company-managed facilities supplying necessary raw materials and products, by 1913, it was considered the largest printing ink works in the world, exporting to Europe, Australia, and Japan.

With the incorporation of the town of Norwood in 1872, there was a conscious effort to attract new industries. Many townspeople understood that the future lay not with dairy farming and agriculture but with large-scale manufacturing, which could provide employment for Norwood's residents and tax money for its municipal needs. One of the first to respond to Norwood's promotional campaign was the New York & New England Railroad Company.

Up to this point, the ownership and maintenance of the ever-increasing network of railroads through the area had been unsatisfactory and confusing. Tiot was only marginally affected by the existing Boston & Worcester line and the Boston & Providence Railroad that cut through the Neponset meadows into Canton. In 1849, the Norfolk County Railroad Company connected the track systems of the Boston & Providence and Boston & Worcester lines and extended the line through Dedham, South Dedham, and Walpole to Blackstone, Rhode Island. Four years later, the newly formed Boston & New York Central Railroad Company absorbed several smaller railroads, including the Norfolk County. Throughout the next two decades, the Boston & New York Central, later called the

The stationery of the George H. Morrill Company ink works indicates how the enterprise had expanded by the early twentieth century. (Courtesy Hansen and Donahue Collection.)

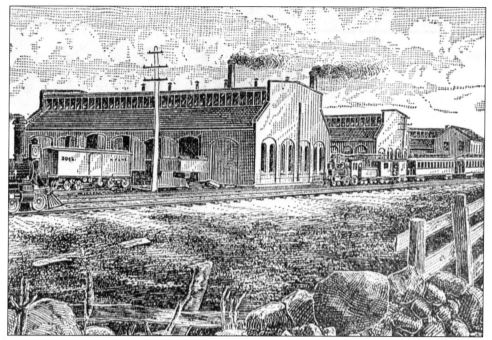

The New York & New England Railroad car shops on Lenox Street were an important employer in the town of Norwood from 1875 to 1903. (Woodcut engraving from the First Resident and Business Directory of Medfield, Walpole, and Norwood, 1884.)

New York, Hartford, & Erie Railroad Company, suffered instability in ownership and financing. Finally, in 1873, the New York & New England Railroad bought out the New York, Hartford & Erie, immediately improving freight and passenger service through Norwood. At about the same time, the repair and maintenance facility of the railroad, situated in Readville, Massachusetts, was destroyed by fire. Within three years, the New York & New England car shops moved into Norwood, where the company erected three substantial buildings on centrally located land along Lenox Street.

Initially, the Norwood facility built and repaired passenger and freight cars, but in 1880, the steam locomotive maintenance unit was brought to town, necessitating the addition of a paint shop, a blacksmith shop, and a special garage. Within ten years, more than 300 skilled artisans and mechanics were employed at the car shops, making the facility a vital component of Norwood's industrial base. By 1897, the property of the New York & New England had been deeded to the New England Railroad Company and, in turn, leased to the New York, New Haven, & Hartford Railroad. Shortly thereafter, beginning in 1903, the car shops were relocated to newly constructed facilities back in Readville, a significant blow to the local economy.

Mindful of the ever-changing business landscape, at the town's annual meeting in 1892, a committee of men, including George S. Winslow, Edmund J. Shattuck, and Lewis Day, was appointed to attract new business and industry to Norwood. Through the efforts of this committee, the Norwood Business Association, later called the Norwood Board of Trade, was established in 1894. Initial membership included the town's most prominent citizens, representatives from town government, industrial and commercial businesses, local clergy, and professional men. One of the first achievements of the association was to bring to town the three independent firms—J.S. Cushing and Company, Berwick and Smith Company, and E. Fleming Company—who together formed the Norwood Press.

Lured by the Norwood Business Association's offer of free land and other inducements, J.S. Cushing and Company moved its composition room and electrotype foundry from Boston in 1894. Since its inception in 1878, the business had been under the watchful eye of its sole proprietor, J. Stearns Cushing, who had made high-grade school books his specialty. Berwick and Smith Company, which operated one of the largest press rooms in the country, arrived in 1895. Having been associated with J.S. Cushing since its founding in 1884, this enterprise was headed by James Berwick and George Harding Smith. A branch of the E. Fleming Company of Boston joined these two concerns in a series of strikingly handsome brick buildings at the intersection of Washington Street and Walnut Avenue in 1897. Later changing its name to C.B. Fleming and Company, Inc., when Charles B. Fleming, grandson of the founder, took over management, this was a press bindery. The addition of this business to the Norwood Press enabled all processes of bookmaking from start to finish to be completed in one large interconnected plant.

While each of the firms maintained their own customer list and separate production orders, a great deal of their collective business derived from complete

This engraving of the Norwood Press complex, located on Washington Street at Walnut Avenue, was the frontispiece of the Resident and Business Directory of Walpole and Norwood, Massachusetts in 1909.

book fabrication. The Norwood Press specialized in scientific, school and college textbooks, Bibles, illustrated books, catalogues, and pamphlets. Collectively, the conglomerate employed some 700 workers during the first two decades of the twentieth century. In 1929, J.S. Cushing and Company added facilities geared to the publication of more popular, less seasonal works of fiction and biography, which, for a time, stabilized the enterprise during and after the Depression. At its peak, the Norwood Press was one of the largest conglomerates of its kind in the country and was widely recognized for the quality and speed of its production.

Enhancing Norwood's reputation as a bookmaking center was the Plimpton Press, an enterprise co-founded by local resident Herbert M. Plimpton and his brother Howard. Born in Walpole, Herbert Plimpton had trained as a compositor, pressman, and binder at a time when bookmaking was largely a process completed by hand labor. In 1882, he founded a book manufacturing company in Boston where he was among the first to advocate for labor and time-saving machinery in the industry. According to several sources, the first folding machines, modern sewing machines, and the first rounding and backing machines were used in Plimpton's Boston plant. Plimpton Press also used the first cover-making machine and invented the first gathering machine. In 1897, attracted by concessions again offered by the Norwood Business Association, Plimpton moved his press work and binding operations to a site east of the railroad tracks on land bounded by Lenox and Nahatan Streets. In 1904, he brought the remainder of his Boston business to Norwood and, by the next year, the firm known as H.M. Plimpton and Company employed about 600. In 1913, the business incorporated as the Plimpton Press and, during the 1920s, employed upwards of 1,000. Its business derived primarily from textbook publishers across the United States and, at its peak, the Plimpton Press could roll 50,000 volumes off its presses daily. Like the Norwood Press, Plimpton Press added fiction, reference works, and religious books to its production schedule in an attempt to offset the seasonal nature of textbook publishing. While the typesetting, presswork, and binding elements of book production were completed in the Plimpton plant, the fabrication of book cloth and binding material was the work of Holliston Mills.

Begun as an adjunct business to the Plimpton Press for the manufacture of book-binding glue, by the late 1890s, Holliston Mills had expanded its interests into the production of book cloth, which was to become its chief product. In their far-sighted quest to advance American book production, Herbert and Howard Plimpton were convinced that American-made fabrics could quickly compete with the British manufacturers who had dominated the industry since its inception. In 1895, this aspect of the business, previously known as the Security Manufacturing Company, was renamed Holliston Mills. Bryant Tolles suggests that the name may have derived from the name of Hollis Plimpton, who became associated with the family business at that time. Although book cloth remained the most important product, Holliston Mills also manufactured window-shade material, broadcloth, and map cloths. Holliston Mills was finally

The Plimpton Press, situated on Lenox Street next to the railroad tracks, arrived in Norwood in 1897 and, at its peak, produced 50,000 volumes daily. (Courtesy Hansen and Donahue Collection.)

incorporated as a separate entity in 1920. In 1926, the firm acquired a facility in Tennessee for finishing and bleaching and an earlier acquisition, the East Braintree Finishing Company, was fitted with machinery for specialty jobs. As the corporation continued to expand and sales offices were opened in Boston, New York, and Chicago, production shifted to these satellite locations. By 1960, active manufacturing had ceased in Norwood and, a decade later, only the executive offices remained in town.

By the late nineteenth century, the industrialization of Norwood was well underway. Bird and Sons, George H. Morrill and Company, the tanneries, the Norwood Press, and the Plimpton Press had changed a small New England village of farms and mills into a bustling community of large-scale manufacturing and production facilities. The presence of these industrial giants, coupled with the efforts of the Norwood Business Association, also resulted in various betterment projects. Norwood's first telephone exchange opened sometime around 1895, in an upstairs room of James Folan's business building, situated next to Village Hall. Shortly thereafter, the exchange moved to the second floor of the Bigelow Block on Washington Street. The town's first bank, the Norwood Co-operative Bank, was established in 1889. Francis Olney Winslow, a well-respected member of the tannery family, was the institution's first president, a position he held for 30 years. Routine bank business was conducted at the Washington Street home of treasurer Dr. Irving S. Fogg until 1918 when space in the Sanborn Block was acquired.

In 1896, Norwood received its first electric car line. Incorporated as the Norfolk Central Street Railway, the trolley ran from the Norwood Press buildings, at Walnut and Washington, to Dedham Square where it continued to Mattapan via the existing Norfolk Suburban Street Railway tracks. When the railroad underpass at Chapel Street was completed, the line was extended through South Norwood to East Walpole. At about the same time, a second trolley line, known by 1901 as the Norfolk & Bristol Street Railway, ran from Guild Square, south along Walpole Street into the town of Walpole. Eventually, arrangements were made that enabled both lines to merge and turn around at the intersection of Washington Street and Railroad Avenue. There were various less than successful attempts to mitigate the resulting congestion. A third trolley line extending from Day Street in downtown Norwood to Canton began service in 1901. It traversed a rather circuitous route along Pleasant, Cross, and Lenox Streets to Broadway, then Day, where it terminated at Day and Washington. As automobile ownership increased, this line was the first trolley to cease operations in March 1918, followed by the Norfolk & Bristol a year later. Finally, in June of 1932, the age of the trolley through town ended when the third line, then known as the Eastern Massachusetts Street Railway, replaced its electric car line service with bus transportation.

The Norwood Business Association also spearheaded other municipal advancements, including the formation of a modern police department in 1896 and an electrical fire alarm system in 1897. Prior to 1896, Norwood was patrolled by two elected constables who worked out of the town offices. In 1879, a lock-up was erected on Market Street, today's Central Street and, in 1903, the building was equipped with steel cells. When the department was officially established, Constable Warren E. Rhoads became the town's first chief of police, and his force was increased to between four and six constables. Although relatively free of major crimes, townspeople welcomed the professionalization of the police force at a time of rapid expansion. Between the years 1890 and 1900, the town's population had grown from 3,732 to 5,480 due mainly to industrial development. In the spring of 1905, Norwood voters agreed to place the police under civil service regulation.

Upon separation from Dedham, the Washington No. 7 and the America No. 10 firehouses had been designated Norwood No. 1 and No. 2 respectively. A board of fire engineers, consisting of Tyler Thayer, John Ellis, and John E. Morse, were appointed to oversee the department. Following the introduction of a water system with hydrant service in 1886, hand engines were replaced. In 1887, a hook-and-ladder and hose house, which the department quickly outgrew, was built on the west side of Market Street. When the brick fire station, with accommodations for police offices on the second floor, was built on the corner of Nahatan and Central Streets in 1905, this brown-shingled structure housed town offices until the present-day municipal building was occupied in 1928.

The households of Norwood prepared for modern conveniences when, in 1905, a four-year study of the advisability of electricity for street and home lighting was completed. In April of that year, an article was placed on the town meeting warrant calling for the construction of a municipally controlled electric light plant, a project that first provided residential and commercial service two years later in August of 1907. That same year, the installation of a sewerage system began, a huge undertaking that resulted in a network of pipes throughout the town and filtration beds on a 14-acre tract of land along the Neponset River. When Norwood became a member of the Metropolitan Sewer System in 1933, these filtration beds were closed. Subsequently, the area was the site of the Norwood Arena and, today, is home to a variety of industrial and commercial buildings. Beginning in 1880, the source of home water, which had previously been ponds, streams, and dug wells, was centralized, utilizing pumping stations at Buckmaster Pond in Westwood and, later, the Ellis field station in the Purgatory Swamp area of Norwood. Despite these facilities, periodic water shortages plagued the town. Consequently, in 1954, Norwood joined the Boston Metropolitan District Commission (MDC) water system and today is part of the Massachusetts Water Resources Authority (MWRA). Since that time, the Buckmaster and Ellis facilities have remained in the town's possession as potential standby, auxiliary, or emergency water sources.

Along with these modern household amenities, turn-of-the-century advocacy resulted in uniform street signs, paved streets, cement sidewalks, and municipal street cleaning. In addition, the Hook was enlarged and modernized with the construction of the Conger Block in 1896, most notably home to Clark's Pharmacy and H.E. Rice and Company Dry Goods Store, and the Bigelow Block in 1900. Farther south, at the corner of East Hoyle and Washington Streets, James

This brick firehouse on Market Street, now Central Street, was erected in 1905 and remained the headquarters of the Norwood Fire Department until the 1960s. (Courtesy Hansen and Donahue Collection.)

Hawkins of Hyde Park built Hawkins Block in 1900. Much like the others, this structure contained street-level storefronts and residential or office space on the second and third stories. Today, the property houses small commercial enterprises such as the Beehive Florist, the *Norwood Bulletin* newspaper offices, and Noonan's Irish Music Shop. The Conger Block was razed in the late twentieth century and the Bigelow Block still stands today on the northeast corner of Day and Washington Streets.

During these years of rapid change, Norwood residents were informed of ongoing activities and improvements by the *Norwood Messenger*. The newspaper began its run in 1895 on a hand press powered by volunteers. It was located in a room upstairs from the Sanborn Brothers hardware store at the corner of Washington Street and Railroad Avenue until the next decade when the facility moved to locations on Cottage and then Vernon Streets. The *Messenger* was not the town's first newspaper, however. The bragging rights for the first Norwood-based journal must go to Francis W. Crooker, who began publication of the *Norwood Advertiser* in 1883. Working out of the old Congregational Church vestry, the *Advertiser* at first competed with the *Norwood Review*, which had been started in 1881 by Charles MacPherson. MacPherson's *Review* was not technically a "Norwood" concern, however, as the newspaper was actually published in Boston and was a duplicate to MacPherson's *Walpole Star*. In 1886, these two small businesses merged and Crooker's paper became the *Norwood Advertiser and Review*. In 1895, E.B. Thorndike purchased the paper from Crooker, moved its headquarters to the Murphy Block at Washington and Day Streets, and continued publication for ten more years until it could no longer compete with the *Messenger*.

Founded by three brothers from West Newbury, Massachusetts—Alfred, Willard, and Edward Ambrose—the *Norwood Messenger* was established in conjunction with the Ambrose Press, the commercial printing arm of the brothers' business. After Edward's death, the remaining two Ambrose brothers dedicated their lives to the *Messenger* and the town. Alfred ("Alec") Ambrose became the primary reporter as well as publisher and editor until the autumn of 1902 when the brothers hired Charles E. Smith, an experienced newspaperman, to cover local events. Smith held this post until 1920, helping to build the reputation and circulation of the newspaper. In 1927, the *Messenger* office moved to Broadway where it occupied space in the old Village Hall, relocated to the corner of Broadway and Nahatan Street by George Willett.

Meanwhile, the Ambrose Press became the really profitable portion of the Ambrose enterprise. By 1920, the facility had begun to print school books in addition to the already wide-ranging business of house publications, catalogues, publicity pieces, and more. The pace continued to increase after the move to Village Hall and under the guardianship of Robert E. Costello, a longtime employee, who purchase the entire operation after Alec Ambrose's death in 1924. It was in 1936, upon Costello's death, that the business was split up and the Ambrose Press, maintaining its name under new owner Carroll Smith of Walpole, moved to a location on Washington Street opposite the Norwood Press buildings.

One of the first notable stories covered by the *Norwood Messenger* in its early years was a muckraking piece on the operation of an illegal "rum-ring" in town. During these years, the sale of liquor was banned in Norwood and many of those who distilled liquor in their homes were arrested and fined. But, according to the Ambrose brothers, hard liquor was being brought into town and distributed at two drugstores through so-called "prescriptions" written up by locals. The perpetrators were some of the town's most respected citizens and the newspaper refused to ignore the practice. By means of this exposé, the *Norwood Messenger* and its editors called attention to emerging inequities. As George Sherlock, editor of the newspaper during the 1970s, wrote in a *Messenger* anniversary edition, the Ambrose brothers "kidded and cajoled, cautioned and criticized, and it was soon recognized that a new influence had entered the community." Thus, with the *Norwood Messenger* as watchdog, the town moved into the twentieth century trying to balance power and money with fairness and equality. But, despite the best of intentions of most residents, with independence and industrial growth had come diversity and disparity, and the town had begun to separate along the lines of class and ethnicity. The influx of wealthy factory owners had changed Norwood's physical, cultural, and civic landscape.

The most obvious and telling transformation occurred in the architecture of the community. What had once been a mismatched array of buildings surrounding the Hook began to display some cohesion in the mid-nineteenth century when the substantial homes of Joseph Day, Joel Baker, Lyman Smith, and L.W. Bigelow were constructed on the west side of Washington Street between Day and Cottage Streets. These stately edifices, home to leather merchant Day, real estate broker Baker, tannery owner Smith, and merchant Bigelow, were set on well-landscaped property, and, along with the First Baptist Church, brought an air of stability and prosperity to the center of town. As the industrialization of Norwood progressed unabated and magnates of the print, ink, and tannery operations became enormously successful, their disproportionate wealth was translated into the construction of ostentatious homes on larger, more spacious estates. The homes of George Harding Smith, J. Stearns Cushing, Herbert M. Plimpton, and the Morrill family were some of the most striking of these mansions.

The three-pronged conglomerate known as the Norwood Press brought to town both George Harding Smith and J. Stearns Cushing. These men quickly became two of Norwood's most prominent citizens and each built a magnificent home on land situated on the west side of Walpole Street about a mile south of the Hook. Smith's rambling stucco and shingle mansion sat on a beautifully landscaped lot overlooking Walpole Street. For a time, after Smith's descendants sold the property in 1929, it became a nursing home. All that remains today is a portion of the front facade, as the structure was converted into an assisted-living facility in the late twentieth century. Cushing's Colonial Revival masterpiece, considered one of the most elegant and beautifully appointed homes in the town, was tucked away at the head of Saunders Road, just west of Smith's mansion. This property became the home of physician James O'Neil and his family

The home of Norwood Press owner J. Stearns Cushing, a remarkable Colonial Revival mansion, which stood at the intersection of Highland Street and Saunders Road, was demolished to make way for new homes in 1996. (Courtesy Bryant F. Tolles.)

during the mid-twentieth century, but was razed to make way for a new housing development in 1996.

Farther south at the corner of Walpole and Chapel Streets stood the exquisite homes of the Plimpton family. The 50-acre site contained two principal mansions, a six-room cottage, a greenhouse, a large barn, a recreational hall built in the form of a ship, and a six-hole golf course. The estate also boasted a sunken garden created by landscape architect Frederick Law Olmsted. After the property passed out of the family's hands, it was subdivided by a local realtor. One of the mansions, bought by the Norwood Post No. 2452 Veterans of Foreign Wars, founded in 1932, burned to the ground in 1957. The other became the headquarters of the Norwood Fraternal Order of Eagles and, after falling into disrepair, was also destroyed by fire in 1976. The site is now home to a housing development and a condominium complex as well as the Grace Episcopal Church and parsonage. A portion of the Olmsted garden was salvaged and restored by the church in conjunction with the Norwood Evening Garden Club.

Nearby, surrounding Winslow's Park, now Disabled American Veterans Memorial Park, were scattered the homes of the Winslow family, including George S. Winslow's home, which was later moved to the corner of Cedar and Chapel Streets; the elder George Winslow's home on Walpole Street, now a medical office building; and Francis O. Winslow's mansard-roofed mansion at the head of Chapel Street. Designed in 1868 by Benjamin Franklin Dwight, a well-known Boston architect, Oak View, as the estate was called, had additions made to it in the 1880s and 1890s. It remains Norwood's finest example of the Second Empire style.

George H. Morrill's 1880 shingle-style home stood on an expansive estate stretching across the intersection of today's Bond, Nichols, Beech, and Winter Streets. It was later purchased by business owner H.E. Rice and, in the

One of two mansions located near Chapel Street belonging to the Plimpton Press family, this magnificent structure became the property of the Veterans of Foreign Wars. It was destroyed by fire in 1957. (Courtesy Hansen and Donahue Collection.)

mid-twentieth century, after being moved and undergoing extensive renovations, it became a nursing home facility. Morrill's son George H. Morrill Jr. built a magnificent stone mansion situated at Bond and Nichols Streets in 1890. It was considered one of Norwood's premiere residences until it too fell into disrepair. When the building was demolished, it was replaced with a development of smaller homes.

Another distinctive house with Morrill connections was the stately home of Edmund J. Shattuck and his wife, Emma Louise Morrill Shattuck, the daughter of Morrill Ink Works owner George H. Morrill. Joining the firm in 1884, Shattuck managed the George H. Morrill Company until his death in 1903. Situated on the southwest corner of Walpole and Winter Streets, the house was razed shortly after the couple's daughter Maud Shattuck died in 1962. The property is now the site of the First Congregational Church. The estate's carriage house was renovated and used as a parish hall by the First Baptist Church, located just south of the First Congregational Church, on the corner of Walpole and Bond Streets. The hall was badly damaged by fire in 2001 and is currently being restored.

The marriage of Emma Morrill to Edmund Shattuck was not the only instance of marriage among the scions of industrial Norwood. Lyman Smith's daughter Anna wed Joseph Day's son Lewis in 1856, making the Winslows, Smiths, and Days a formidable force in the community. Meanwhile, George H. Morrill's daughter Alice married into the Plimpton family, thereby binding the Morrills, Plimptons, and Shattucks closer together. In addition, the two daughters of tannery owner Francis O. Winslow married George Willett and Frank Allen, men who were each to have a lasting impact on twentieth-century Norwood. As might be imagined, the lifestyle supported by this wealth distanced these industrialists from the rest of the community. Able to afford private schools, world travel, and all the available luxuries, these families had little in common even with their middle-class neighbors, while the maintenance of their properties depended on household staffs of maids, cooks, gardeners, and liverymen drawn from the ranks of the town's working class.

Some of these class distinctions were reflected in a cultural transformation within the town. Community leaders, seeking camaraderie among their own kind, founded a variety of cultural organizations. The oldest local organization, still active today, is the Orient Lodge of the Ancient Free and Accepted Masons. Founded in 1861 and officially chartered in 1862, the Masons first held their meetings in Village Hall. Membership consisted of many of the town's founding fathers, including Joseph Day, Joseph Sumner, and James Hartshorn. In 1868, the Masons purchased Village Hall and utilized its assembly room until 1915 when the building was sold to George Willett. The Lodge next met in the Conger Hall until 1917 when their temple on Day Street was dedicated. This building remains in use today. Self-described as "a charitable, benevolent, educational and religious society," the Lodge has always allowed other Masonic bodies and kindred groups to meet in the temple.

In 1886, the Independent Order of Odd Fellows was instituted with ten charter members. This popular organization purchased the old Tiot Tavern, or Norwood House, and met there beginning in 1887. In 1911, they purchased property on the corner of Vernon and Washington Streets and erected a building that still stands today. The Odd Fellows, whose functions were largely social in nature, was a society of benevolence and friendship and shared many members and beliefs with the Masons.

The hall in the Odd Fellows Building, located at the corner of Vernon and Washington Streets, was utilized by a number of civic and religious organizations. The relocated Lyman Smith house can be seen to the rear. (Courtesy Hansen and Donahue Collection.)

Another organization founded in the latter part of the nineteenth century, the Norwood Literary Society, had strikingly different concerns. The "Chautauqua Literary and Scientific Circle," formed in 1883, quickly became one of the town's most active cultural groups. Headed by Francis O. Winslow, an esteemed member of the Winslow tannery family, the organization changed its name to the Literary Club or Society ten years later. Limiting its ranks to 50, membership was a who's who of prominent Norwood families. The group sponsored poetry and book discussions, lectures, original story telling, dramatic and musical productions, and a much anticipated annual outing.

In 1901, members of the Literary Society noted that "an effort should be made to form a Norwood Historical Society, while we had people among us to tell its history, and give us relics of the past." Six years later, the Norwood Historical Society was officially organized. The historical society immediately began to accumulate artifacts, genealogical notes, photographs, and memorabilia related to the development of the town. For almost 30 years, meetings were held at the homes of members. Although collecting and preserving the history of the entire town of Norwood was the stated goal of the group, until quite late in the twentieth century, the bulk of materials collected related to the commercial development of the town and the families of the industrial magnates. A large percentage of the community was not reflected in the collection or the membership any more than they were represented in the Masons, Odd Fellows, or Literary Society. For a variety of reasons, ethnic groups, including the Irish, Italian, Lithuanian, Finnish, and German populations, established their own benevolent, fraternal, and social clubs.

"Oak View," the home of tannery owner Francis O. Winslow, is pictured here shortly after the mansion was completed and before several additions in succeeding decades. (Picturesque Norwood photo.)

Called "The Pines" by its owner, George H. Morrill Jr., this castle-like structure was built in 1890 and demolished after falling into disrepair in the mid-twentieth century. (Courtesy Norwood Historical Society.)

Through the generosity of Mr. and Mrs. George H. Morrill, the gap between community factions began to be bridged with the building of the Morrill Memorial Library. The roots of this public institution extend back to the early nineteenth century. Inspired by Reverend Jabez Chickering's willingness to share his own personal book collection, members of his Congregational Church parish founded a circulating library in 1800. Called the South Dedham Parish Library, the organization had a constitution, by-laws, and stockholders. This library continued to function, housed in parishioners' homes until the 1860s when the collection was relocated to a small third-floor room of Village Hall. At that point, the library had grown to nearly 1,500 volumes. By 1873, however, interest in and financial support of this chiefly private library had somewhat waned. In March 1873, within one year of Norwood's incorporation, this collection was offered to the town as a gift with the condition that the books be circulated among the general public free of charge. One month later, the offer was accepted, a six-member library board of trustees was chosen, and a sum of $300 was appropriated for the library's continued support.

By the autumn of 1873, the collection had been moved to the second floor of Hartshorn's Block, over Francis Tinker's drugstore, and the town's first free public library was open for business. With the expansion of the collection to some 5,000 volumes, the library returned to more spacious quarters in Village Hall in 1886. Despite modest financial support from the town, monies to sustain the library were a constant concern. Throughout the 1880s and 1890s, activities were sponsored to raise funds and public awareness. Some patrons even excitedly discussed the possibility of the eventual construction of a library building. Then, in 1897, two of the town's most significant benefactors stepped forward, offering to build a library. Grieving from the loss of their 23-year-old daughter to typhoid fever in 1896, George H. and Louisa J. Morrill saw the library as a way to establish a permanent memorial to her. The town accepted this magnanimous philanthropic gesture and a Romanesque Revival–style structure, a near duplicate to the Lithgow Library in Augusta, Maine, was erected. In February of 1898, the Sarah Bond Morrill Memorial Library was dedicated.

Constructed from Maine granite, the building featured a red-tile roof, eyebrow dormer windows, and a distinctive entrance arch. The interior of the building was equally impressive with mahogany paneling and finely detailed furnishings and fixtures. Under the direction of head librarian Jane A. Hewitt, who held the position for 41 years, the Morrill Memorial Library became the cultural center of the community. The Morrill family maintained its personal dedication to the institution as well. An addition to the building was made possible by a bequest of Mrs. Alice Morrill Plimpton, daughter of the donors, in 1928 and the Morrill's granddaughter Maud Shattuck served on the board of trustees from 1918 until 1956.

While the generous donation of the library building by the Morrills was an extremely significant event in and of itself, the gesture also seemed to usher in a new era of civic responsibility. That same year, Winslow Park was deeded to the town by the Winslow family and, within a decade, two new elementary schools bore the names of successful industrialists with the opening of the Edmund J. Shattuck School in 1903 and the Winslow School in 1907. Still, the family that may have demonstrated the highest level of dedication to the community, at least until the era of George F. Willett, was the Lewis Day family. Together, Lewis and Anna Smith Day and their only child Fred Holland Day did much to preserve the town's heritage and contribute to its future.

The Morrill Memorial Library was built and presented to the town in 1898 by George H. and Louise Morrill in memory of their daughter Sara Bond Morrill. (Courtesy Hansen and Donahue Collection.)

3. The Age of Influence: F. Holland Day and W. Cameron Forbes

Fred Holland Day (1864–1933) was the only child of leather merchant Lewis Day and Anna Smith Day, daughter of Lyman Smith of the Winslow and Smith tanneries. Somewhat ironically, he grew to be a leader in the movement to restore idealism, beauty, and hand craftsmanship during the age of industrialization and modernization. Ironic because it was this very industrialism that brought his family the wealth that enabled him to pursue his artistic goals in the fields of publishing and photography. "If there is a theme that lends understanding to Day's life," writes photographic historian Verna Curtis, "it would be his loyalty and dedication to his home and the ideals and achievements of his country." Day was, first and foremost, a local historian, devoted to the preservation of the history of his family and community. Even his last will and testament states that "It is the general purpose of this will to be of assistance to persons and societies interested in the history of Old Dedham," which, of course, included Norwood. In this worthy endeavor, he was following in the footsteps of his parents and grandparents before him.

Anna Smith and Lewis Day had, coincidentally, been born in the same house in South Dedham, situated on the Wrentham Road, now Walpole Street, the first regular stagecoach route between Boston and Providence. Built by John Smith, the early tannery owner, by the 1830s, it had become the home of Smith's son Lyman and his wife Melinda Guild Smith. The house was temporarily occupied by Smith's friend and business associate Joseph Day and his wife Hannah Rhoades Day, when their son Lewis was born in 1835. Smith and his family returned to the house before their daughter Anna was born a year later. The Smith-Day association was one of long-standing. Born in nearby Walpole, Massachusetts, Joseph Day was a direct descendant of Ralph Day, an early Dedham settler. Ralph Day had emigrated from England in 1630, arrived in Dedham, and married Susan Fairbanks, daughter of Jonathan Fairbanks. Ralph's grandson Jeremiah moved to Walpole in 1729 and the family remained there for

This view of Bullard Farm, home of the Lewis Day family, was taken around 1870 and shows the house, carriage house, and tent erected for Fred Day's birthday party. (Courtesy Morrill Memorial Library.)

several generations. Like Lyman Smith, Joseph Day received village schooling until the age of 16 when he left home. He learned the art of currying leather, dressing and coloring leather after it has been tanned, from William Pratt of Roxbury, and was employed in South Dedham with John and Lyman Smith when he was 20. Restless and unsettled, Day moved to Rhode Island and, for four years, worked as a journeyman in the trade in Providence and Pawtucket. When he returned to South Dedham in 1830, he tried his hand at manufacturing wrapping paper with Isaac Ellis in a small factory on the shores of Ellis Pond, near the Walpole–South Dedham border.

In 1830, he married Hannah Rhoades, granddaughter of Eliphalet Rhoades and Mercy Holland, who were also Lyman Smith's grandparents. In the growing community that Tiot had become, Day's marriage to Lyman Smith's cousin brought him securely under the influence of the successful Smith family. By 1833, he had returned to his first trade, opening a shop for currying and selling leather near the Hook. Ten years later, he became a leather dealer in Boston. A devout Universalist with an ecumenical spirit, Joseph Day served as a representative to the General Court in 1843 and 1844, and was a senator from Norfolk County in 1856 and 1857. During his senate term, he was an active member of the Committee on Prisons and Reformatory Institutions, a commitment continued by his daughter-in-law Anna Smith Day in later decades. Day was also a Mason and was instrumental in the founding of South Dedham's own lodge in 1861. A history, written on the 100th anniversary of the organization, called him, "Perhaps the outstanding man in the formation of the Lodge." He held the position of treasurer of the group from its inception until his death. When he died in 1876, Day was eulogized by the Reverend George Hill in

The Universalist, the official newspaper of the Universalist Society in Boston. Hill called Day, "a well developed, good and true man" who was "as open-hearted as he was open-handed." It had been Joseph Day, in fact, who, in 1856, ensured, through the use of his own funds, that the Roman Catholic congregation was able to purchase the Universalist's first meeting house on Washington Street and establish their own parish.

For their part, Lewis Day and Anna Smith had known one another all their lives, having been raised in the same village and Universalist congregation. Lewis's formal education, limited to village schooling, ended in 1853 when, at 18, he joined his father in the leather business. Three years later, the small, dark, quiet young man married the 20-year-old daughter of his father's old friend Lyman Smith. Much like his father before him, Lewis Day was a keen businessman. After taking over the Day family business in 1864, the year of Fred Day's birth, Lewis became one of the wealthiest men in South Dedham. Still, he was best known for his congeniality and modesty. Following in his own father's footsteps, Lewis was accepted into the local lodge of Masons, eventually rising to the 32nd degree. In the 1870s, he was elected as a representative to the state legislature and took on a leadership role in the Universalist Church of Norwood. When a devastating fire destroyed the meetinghouse in 1884, Lewis chaired the re-building committee

Extensively renovated in the 1890s, the Day house is today the headquarters of the Norwood Historical Society, which purchased the mansion after Fred Day's death in 1933. (Courtesy Bryant F. Tolles.)

and used his own monies to see to it that the building and its bell tower were completed on schedule.

Lewis was joined in his generosity and dedication to the community by his wife Anna. Born in 1836, Anna had lost her own mother, Melinda Guild Smith, when she was only ten. Under the guidance of her hard-working, laboring father and his second wife, Ann Joy Smith, Anna was educated in Tiot schools and grew into a gracious and compassionate woman. She was, by all accounts, without prejudice or pretension. Fred Day's own liberality and generosity, while inherited from both parents, can be traced to Anna in particular. One family friend, in fact, predicted that Fred would eventually "become like his mother and look at everything from a philanthropic standpoint." Believing, like her father, unquestionably in the Universalist philosophies of equality and social responsibility, Anna led by example. A volunteer worker at the North End Union and a trustee of the Westborough Insane Hospital, she also lent her name and financial support to a number of worthy causes. Known for her sweet personality and acts of kindness, Anna treated all who entered her household like family, making them feel welcome and at ease.

Their family connections and community spirit brought the Days into the center of many significant town events. It was in their home, an impressive mansard-style edifice called Bullard Farm, built for them in 1859 by Tyler Thayer, that the 1872 celebratory reception commemorating Norwood's founding was held. Guests on that occasion included dignitaries from the mother town of Dedham and the

This dramatic view from the third-floor balcony of the Day house captures a portion of the balconies, interior windows, and balustrades in the great hall. (Courtesy Hansen and Donahue Collection.)

The interior of the remodeled Day house includes stucco walls, exquisite paneling, and a striking stairway in its central great hall. (Courtesy Hansen and Donahue Collection.)

governor of the Commonwealth. Fourteen years later, as Lewis presided over the dedication of the new Universalist Church, Anna donated a large circular stained-glass window depicting the baptism of Christ, dedicated to the memory of her parents. Newspaper records also indicate that Fred was preparing a memorial tribute of his own, assembling a collection of the portraits of all 29 pastors who had served the parish since its foundation in 1827. Fred also had participated in fundraising for the new building in 1885 by presenting a well-received lecture with stereopticon and lantern views in Village Hall.

By the time of the Universalist Church dedication, the younger Day was 22 years old and embarking on his own remarkable career. As might be anticipated, both Lewis and Anna had doted on their only child. He did not attend public schools, but instead had a personal nurse and early tutor. By the time he was 12, Fred was attending Mrs. Charles E. Morse's private school. There he was joined by the children of the Winslow, Morrill, and Morse families, all descendants of Tiot's prosperous industrialists. Along with the standard curriculum, Fred was enrolled in music, singing, and oil painting instruction, the latter becoming a particular favorite. Beginning in 1881, he was enrolled at Chauncy Hall, a liberal preparatory high school located near Copley Square in Boston, a place known for its encouragement of art as well as literature and history. At Chauncy Hall, Fred's imagination became engaged and his confidence grew. By the time he graduated in 1883, he had earned a medal for excellence in the study of literature, was the president of the Chauncy Lyceum, and had developed a passion for the arts.

After a brief stint as a depository secretary in the Boston branch of A.S. Barnes and Company, booksellers, Day turned his attention and talent to art, publishing, and photography. With a group of like-minded friends, he promoted a new Renaissance focusing on individualism, craftsmanship, and beauty at a time when industrialism, modernization, and mass production had become the norm.

He helped to publish two short-lived periodicals, *The Mahogany Tree* and *The Knight Errant*, before founding the Copeland & Day publishing firm along with friend Herbert Copeland. Supported primarily by the Day family's considerable wealth, Copeland & Day remained in business for six years, publishing some 99 works of fiction, poetry, and history. Unlike the books manufactured at the Norwood and Plimpton Press complexes, the Copeland and Day partnership specialized in small runs of exquisitely produced volumes featuring unique graphic design and illustrations.

Closer to home, in June of 1891, after considerable planning, the Day family vacated their Norwood estate and had the then 30-year-old mansion totally remodeled. Within two years, their once stately but conventional home had been turned into an eclectic English Tudor-style mansion with Arts and Crafts influences. There was nothing quite like it in Norwood. Standing at the crest of Day Street, overlooking Joseph Day's home on Washington Street and the town beyond, the edifice featured almost Gothic overhangs, a wide veranda, and unsurpassed exterior detail. Inside, the mansion was even more distinctive with interior windows, a three-storied great hall, and multi-level library among its features. Now on the National Register of Historic Places, the home remains a showplace as the headquarters of the Norwood Historical Society, which purchased the building after Fred Day's death.

This view of the Dedham Historical Society Museum and exhibit was taken in 1887 by Fred Day shortly after the town's 250th anniversary. (Courtesy Dedham Historical Society.)

While the Day family could not have anticipated the society's purchase of the home, their commitment to the town and its heritage is a matter of record. At an early age, Fred Day began to collect historical artifacts, including plates, furniture, and clothing. This interest in local history can be traced to his discovery of an 1827 history of the town of Dedham in the papers of his great grandfather. In writing to the author's son Erastus Worthington in 1886, Day stated the following:

> Although my father and mother before me were born and bred in the South Dedham Parish I must acknowledge myself very ignorant of our mother town. During the coming Spring and Summer I hope to make myself better acquainted with not only your living and your dead but their habitations.

Day made good on that promise and continued to add to his archive of local history documents, photographs, and genealogical records throughout his lifetime. A few of his more significant acquisitions were the pine cabinet used by Reverend Jabez Chickering to hold Tiot's first library and a fireplace salvaged prior to the demolition of the Joel Everett house on Pleasant Street that was installed in the library of the Day's renovated home. Lewis Day encouraged his son's interest in local history and genealogical research as a member and volunteer at the Dedham Historical Society.

This photograph of John Fiske, George Clark, and oxen was taken by Fred Day in 1887 to preserve the memory of a vanishing lifestyle. (Courtesy Norwood Historical Society.)

It was, in fact, this abiding concern for preservation and history that drew Fred Day into the world of photography. Beginning in the mid-1880s, he took up the camera initially as a documentary tool to capture images of historic sites, homes, and a vanishing lifestyle. In September of 1886, during Dedham's 250th anniversary celebration, he photographed a few homesteads, the Old Powder House, and views of Dedham's historical display. As his interest in photography deepened, his work shifted to artistic photography. By the late 1890s, Day became a respected leader of the emerging Pictorialist movement within photography, advocating for the recognition of photography as an art and defending the right of photographers to include the nude and the sacred subject in their work. He became a generous mentor, providing financial and educational assistance to countless young people as a settlement house volunteer in the 1880s, a family visitor under the auspices of the Boston Children's Aid Society in the 1890s, and an advisor and colleague to aspiring artists during the first two decades of the twentieth century. One of his most famous protégés was Kahlil Gibran. Rescued by Day from a life as a street vendor, Gibran went on to become a well-known artist and author of *The Prophet*.

Even at the height of his artistic career, Day's commitment to his community remained steadfast. In 1903, along with his parents, he oversaw the construction of the Chapel of St. Gabriel the Archangel in Norwood's Highland Cemetery. Designed by the architectural firm of Cram, Goodhue, and Ferguson, two members of which, Ralph Adams Cram and Bertram Grosvenor Goodhue, were close friends of Fred Holland Day's, the neo-Gothic chapel's elegance depends on its simple proportions rather than a richness of decoration. Materials included a seam-faced granite and limestone exterior and white marble interior trim. The building contains the chapel itself as well as a chantry where tombs for the family were placed. On May 30, 1903, the chapel was officially dedicated to the memory of Joseph and Hannah Rhoades Day and Lyman and Melinda Guild Smith with the moving words, "They were among those who comprised the small family of the early town of South Dedham, who were interested in its prosperity and its moral welfare. Here they lived and labored and died and we have entered into their labors." As if to reaffirm the importance of its connection to the town's history, the solid doors of the chapel were constructed from wood salvaged from an eighteenth-century Tiot farmhouse and barn. At the direction of the family, the chapel is available to all residents of the town at no charge for funeral services, irrespective of religious beliefs. Along with the donation of the building, the Days made a special bequest to the town to cover maintenance expenses in perpetuity.

After several decades spent in Boston, London, and a summer home in Maine, Fred Day returned to Norwood to care for his ailing mother in 1917 and devoted much of the remainder of his life to local history and genealogical research. Day also became a primary source for the historical writings of W.W. Everett, popular local historian, whose articles appeared in the *Norwood Messenger* throughout the 1930s. Everett often credited Day's research and collection in his columns. At the time of Day's death, in November of 1933, a *Norwood Messenger* article, probably

The Chapel of St. Gabriel the Archangel was built by the Day family and presented to the town of Norwood for use by all resident at no charge for funeral services, irrespective of religious beliefs.

written by Everett himself, remarks on Day's individuality of thought, brilliancy of mind, and artistic temperament. Although noting his international celebrity, it is Day's abiding commitment to the history of the early settlers of Norwood that was deemed his "life's work." Before his death, Day had been gathering material for a proposed history of Tiot, but did not live to see the work completed. He did, however, make significant contributions to two historical projects. In 1927, the First Universalist Church commemorated "a century of service," and Day's historical knowledge and actual artifacts made the celebration a success. His work was so important to the celebration that the program itself stated:

> It is the desire of the Pageant Committee to express a special word of thanks to Mr. Fred H. Day for his invaluable assistance. It would have been impossible to accomplish what we have without his unlimited knowledge of local history and persons. But as well as giving that, he has contributed of his time and advice on other matters, has loaned us objects of historical interest, and contributed the facsimile programs which are to be used at the Sunday morning service. If this celebration be in any wise successful, much of the credit must be given him.

One year later, in 1928, when the Norwood Memorial Municipal Building was dedicated, it was the research by Fred Day that resulted in the town's tribute to veterans. Although by this time a bedridden invalid, Day undertook the painstaking

Fred Holland Day was a highly influential publisher and photographer at the turn of the twentieth century. This photograph of Day was taken by Frederick Hollyer, an English photographer. (Courtesy Norwood Historical Society.)

task of compiling a comprehensive list of those who had served the parish and the town in all armed conflicts to date, including the Colonial Wars. Although seemingly unacknowledged at the time, Day's correspondence makes it clear how proud he was to contribute in some small part to the commemoration.

In keeping with their lifelong generosity and concern for those less fortunate, Lewis and Anna Day jointly agreed to bestow on the town one final gift. Their probate documents state that once a small number of personal bequests were made and their son was taken care of, it was their intention to found and endow a home for the elderly who needed financial assistance. It was to be called "The Lewis and Anna M. Day Home for the Aged in Norwood, Inc." All of their personal and real property, including their Norwood mansion, was to be sold and the trustees were to purchase land and erect buildings "of a substantial nature for the comfort and convenience of those who would live there." It was a final gesture to perpetuate within the community the benefits of their life's work. Although the Home for the Aged was never built, the monies accumulated were donated to local institutions charged with the care of the aged poor.

As his own death approached, Fred Day followed the example of his philanthropic parents. First, his extensive and invaluable collection of materials relating to the life and work of the poet John Keats was sent to the Keats Homestead in England. Second, letters from his close friend the poet Louise Imogen Guiney, along with a collection of his own photographic work, was donated to the Library of Congress. Both of these bequests were made anonymously, although the content of each made it quite easy to surmise whom the donor must have been. The bulk of his estate, including both tangible property and monetary holdings, was placed in a trust to be known as the Joseph Day Trust and bequeathed to the Dedham Historical Society. There was one condition, however. If, prior to January 1970, the Norwood Historical Society could acquire and maintain a building for one full year, then the Dedham Historical Society could terminate the Joseph Day Trust and transfer the funds, investments, and property of historic and genealogical interest to the Norwood Historical Society "for the purpose of stimulating and sustaining interest in the history of the area now within the limits of the Town of Norwood." If the Norwood Historical Society could not fulfill these conditions by January 1970, all the assets and property of the Joseph Day Trust would become a permanent part of the Dedham Historical Society.

Having languished since its inception in 1907, members of the Norwood Historical Society were aroused by this incentive and, in June of 1934, financed the purchase of the Day house from the trustees of the Lewis and Anna M. Day Home for the Aged in Norwood, Inc. One year later, as stipulated in Fred Day's will, the society received the proceeds from the Joseph Day Trust, allowing the society to pay off the mortgage and to acquire the priceless collection of local history memorabilia, documents, photographs, and artifacts assembled by Fred Day during his lifetime. Spurred on by this acquisition, the historical society briefly took on new life and enthusiasm. Most notably, during the late 1930s, the society sponsored the Lewis Day School of Vocational Education. Under its auspices, classes were held in pottery, drawing, graphic design, painting, and textile handwork. Annual art exhibits at the Day House showcased the work of the school's students.

Still a viable organization today, the Norwood Historical Society, nearing its centennial year, continues to maintain the Day House, remarkably intact with period furnishings, and to underwrite programs of historical interest. The society and the town received considerable attention in 2001 when the Museum of Fine Arts, Boston held a retrospective of F. Holland Day's photographic work. This major exhibition, recognized by the *Boston Globe* as one of the year's ten best in Boston, included over 100 of Day's photographs, re-establishing his international reputation and celebrity.

Just off Upland Road, a short distance from the Day House, stands a second distinctive Norwood home with a storied past. W. Cameron Forbes was not a local historian or artist but an athlete, polo enthusiast, and diplomat. Yet, his career, falling as it did during the years of Day's celebrity, exemplifies influence of a different sort, and his home, although still standing today, tells the tale not of historic preservation, but of industrial change and adaptation.

William Cameron Forbes (1870–1959) was born in Milton, Massachusetts on May 21, 1870, to a prominent and wealthy Massachusetts family. His father, William Hathaway Forbes, was an early president of the American Bell Telephone Company, and his grandfather founded the Boston banking house J.M. Forbes and Company in 1838. Cameron Forbes's mother, Edith Emerson Forbes, was the daughter of Ralph Waldo Emerson, the famed Concord poet and philosopher. Although only 12 at the time of Emerson's death, Forbes later recalled holding his grandfather's hand and accompanying him to church as a small boy.

Forbes was educated at Milton Academy and graduated from Harvard University in 1892, one year after F. Holland Day's business partner, Herbert Copeland. Unlike Copeland, Day, and their friends, however, Forbes was not devoted to the arts; his fields of interest were business, politics, and sports. While at Harvard he played on his class football team, but despite great enthusiasm, never made the varsity. In 1894, however, he became the coach of Harvard's freshman team and, in 1897 and 1898, he was head coach of Harvard varsity football. Perhaps a testament to his skill and dedication, his team was undefeated during the 1898 season.

W. Cameron Forbes served as governor-general of the Philippines (1909–1913) and United States ambassador to Japan (1930–1932) and built a remarkable mansion off Upland Road. (Courtesy Norwood Historical Society.)

At the same time he was scaling the heights of Ivy League football, Forbes was beginning his business career as a clerk with the Boston brokerage firm of Jackson and Curtis. By 1897, he had moved on to Stone and Webster, where he specialized in the development and management of utility and railway properties. Upon the death of his grandfather in 1898, he became a partner in J.M. Forbes and Company. In addition to the increased responsibilities that partnership brought him, Forbes served as director to an ever-widening number of institutions, including the American Telephone and Telegraph Company, Arthur D. Little, Inc., the First National Bank of Boston, and the United Fruit Company. He also began to express an interest in government affairs on an international level, offering his services to the Panama Canal Commission.

Although he was not given that appointment, a few years later Forbes was asked by President Theodore Roosevelt to join the Philippine Commission, a governing body set up to establish a civil government in the Philippine territories following the Spanish-American War. As a member of the commission, Forbes supervised an enormous range of public and commercial activities. His responsibilities included police, post office, telegraph, and lighthouse services, as well as railroad construction and port improvements. He was also chairman of the committee that organized a merchant marine service for the islands. In 1908, Roosevelt appointed him vice-governor and, a year later, President Taft made Forbes governor-general of the Philippine Islands, a post he held for four years. Among Forbes's most successful actions during his time as governor-general were road, port, and artesian well development and the establishment of a self-governing penal colony at Iwahig. Forbes also devoted much of his time to educational, agricultural, and industrial improvements in the Philippines.

During this service, Forbes became fascinated by the variety and beauty of the woods available on the islands, so much so that he used 12 remarkable woods in the interior design and furniture of his Norwood home. The Forbes Mansion, as it has come to be called, was built between 1914 and 1916 on land acquired by Forbes from the estate of Henry O. Peabody. Originally known as the King-Gay farm, the Forbes estate was self supporting. It covered hundreds of acres, and included seven houses, five farms, a dairy, greenhouses, beef cattle, an apple orchard, cider mill, and sawmill. Forbes allowed area residents to hunt, camp, and skate within the estate. Many more Norwood natives came to the garage on the property to buy apples and cider produced on the premises. In addition, the sawmill provided work for local laborers during the winter months when pine trees were cut down to make apple boxes.

Cameron Forbes's main house was a palatial 30-room Georgian Revival masterpiece composed of a long rectangular nine-bay main structure, flanked by wings and end pavilions. Its massive chimneys, monumental columns, and semi-circular portico inspired a Massachusetts Historical Commission surveyor to characterize the mansion as "a rather adventurous and successful marriage of Early Georgian Revival form with a center pavilion and portico reminiscent of the brand of Classicism popular in England during the late 18th century." The

This dairy farm building on the north side of Prospect Street, shown here just after completion, was part of W. Cameron Forbes's working farm. (Courtesy Norwood Historical Society.)

grounds included impeccably groomed lawns and woodlands that allowed for an unsurpassed view of the Great Blue Hill in the distance and the Canton Meadows in the foreground. To the west, Forbes had a hill leveled to construct a polo field on the property. A noted polo expert, Forbes played the sport for more than 40 years, even writing a widely read textbook *As to Polo* in 1911. Both the matches held there and the wealthy participants were, quite naturally, the subject of much curiosity and discussion among the local population. The interior of the residence even featured a "pony parlor," for the indoor display of ponies, and several suites of dormitory-type rooms for polo club members. The pony room was finished in a nearly indestructible Philippine wood called molave.

The rest of the interior of the mansion was remarkable as well. The central hall, two stories high, with a magnificent wooden balustrade around the second level, was finished in the brown-hued acle wood, while a lavish suite reserved for special guests was paneled in a rich, dark red tindalo. Forbes's own bedroom contained an extremely durable first-grade aromatic wood called calamansana. One of the panels near the bed could be lowered to serve as a table and a dumbwaiter and private stairway connected the chamber to a kitchenette immediately below. Much wealthier than any other Norwood family, including the Winslows, Plimptons, and Morrills, Forbes circled the world four times and often traveled to Europe and to Central and South America. He spent his summers on Naushon, a family-owned island off Cape Cod, and made frequent visits to another familial property, a ranch in Wyoming.

Upon his return from the Philippines, Forbes donated a collection of Philippine weapons, basket work, headdresses, and costumes to the Peabody Museum at Harvard, became an overseer of Harvard University, and resumed his directorship of a number of corporations. After a series of appointments during the 1920s to investigate conditions in the Philippines and Haiti as a result of American occupancy, Forbes, at 60, was named ambassador to Japan by President Herbert Hoover in 1930. He resigned the post two years later after the Japanese invaded Manchuria. Throughout the 1930s, Forbes remained active within polo circles and maintained an interest in local affairs. In 1940, the Norwood Chamber of Commerce held a testimonial to Forbes, thanking him for his cooperation and encouragement over the years. Among those thanking the longtime honorary member of the chamber was historian Charles Francis Adams and former governor and Norwood resident Frank G. Allen.

Until advancing years and ill health forced him to resign, Forbes remained on the boards of several corporations and for many years he also served as chairman of the board of trustees of the Carnegie Institute of Washington and a trustee of the Hampton Institute in Virginia. In 1950, at the age of 80, Forbes broke up his estate. Garelick Brothers bought the dairy business and much of the rest of the land was sold piecemeal. Forbes donated his Norwood mansion, with polo fields and stables, to Harvard University. Nine years later, he died in his apartment at the Hotel Vendome in Boston.

This 1920 aerial photograph of the Forbes mansion and grounds includes a view of the polo field behind the house. (Courtesy Hansen and Donahue Collection.)

This was not the end of the relationship between the mansion that Forbes built and the town of Norwood, however. In 1955, the house and surrounding property was acquired by the United Fruit Company and was converted into a research laboratory. The semi-secluded estate was chosen primarily because of its proximity to leading Boston universities where scientists and facilities were available for consultation. After new greenhouses and outbuildings were constructed, it became the largest banana research facility outside the tropics. At its peak, it housed 45 scientists and technicians who were recruited from all over the country to work in six specially designed laboratories. The United Fruit greenhouses contained some 1,000 plants, many of which grew to between 20 and 30 feet high. Studies were conducted on numerous topics, including a complete study of the banana plant itself, its growing habits, environmental influences, the nature of the pests and blights which affect it, and the problems of shipping ripe fruit. The third floor of Forbes's former home, where once political dignitaries, polo enthusiasts, and people of great wealth had enjoyed the comforts of this exquisite structure, was now the entomology room, filled with butterflies, cockroaches, poisonous spiders, and a host of other insects under study.

The complex system of wiring, plumbing, and heating within the estate was modified, and temperature, light, and humidity factors were closely monitored. Because the banana plants could not tolerate temperatures below 56 degrees, emergency generators were set up to take over in case of a power failure. A new, shorter species of banana plant, which made harvesting easier, was developed at the Norwood facility. As the company moved toward diversification, United Fruit also developed and patented freeze-dried fruits, vegetables, and shrimp for Kellogg's and Campbell Soup Company at the mansion.

In 1967, following two years of negotiations with town officials and residents, the Polaroid Corporation purchased the Forbes site from United Fruit. Founded in 1937, Polaroid was, even then, a worldwide leader in photography and instant imaging. During the next two years, a modern manufacturing plant was constructed on the property. Several sources commended the corporation for its sensitive conversion of the mansion into corporate offices, retaining much of the irreplaceable wood paneling and many of the distinctive architectural features of the building. With considerable attention also paid to the preservation of the surrounding natural environment, the locale continued to be the most attractively landscaped industrial complex in Norwood. In the late 1990s, while Polaroid maintained a manufacturing presence on the property, the mansion and adjoining land were sold to Putnam Investments, a global money management firm, which houses offices and a training site on the property. This most recent change in the mansion's ownership is both reflective of the country's economic shift from production to information services and, in some respects, a return to the investment and banking roots of its creator W. Cameron Forbes.

4. IMMIGRATION AND GROWTH

More than 150 years after its first permanent settlers arrived, Tiot remained almost exclusively Anglo-Saxon Protestant, primarily Congregationalist. By the mid-nineteenth century, however, that began to change. Initially, workers arrived to build the Norfolk County Railroad; later, many remained to fill positions in the factories in and around South Dedham. The earliest group, according to Bryant Tolles, "almost entirely Irish, numbered approximately 75 and came from Counties Clare and Mayo in southwestern Ireland." By a coincidence of fate, just as the railroad arrived and factories sought laborers in South Dedham, the Irish were being driven from their home country by a disastrous multi-year potato blight and subsequent famine. Upon their arrival, there was little in the way of housing in the community. Consequently, many of these Irish pioneers found themselves without a place to live until Moses Guild converted his old wagon barn into a tenement.

Guild, who lived in the former Balch parsonage, had become fairly prosperous as the owner of a fleet of freight wagons running between Boston and Providence over the Norfolk and Bristol turnpike. He stored his wagons and equipment in a two-story structure on the corner of Washington and Guild Streets, near today's park. Sometime between 1840 and 1850, Guild began to phase out his business and rented the wagon house to O.W. Fiske, who turned the building into a playing card factory, powered by steam, rather than water. Known from that time on as the Old Steam Mill, the building became vacant when Fiske moved to Bedford, Massachusetts. Guild then renovated the structure into a tenement house for incoming Irish families. According to legend, both floors of the building were divided into 12-by-12-foot rooms, lighting was from whale oil lamps and lanterns, a bucket-well provided water, and the sanitary facilities consisted of a sole privy for several families. Among those residing for a time in the old steam mill were familiar Norwood Irish names, including Pendergast, Cuff, Casey, and Oldham. After a few years of steady employment and frugality, most tenants moved into homes of their own. The two neighborhoods where the Irish primarily settled in small cottage-style houses came to be called "Dublin," located along Railroad Avenue, west of Washington Street, and "Cork City," radiating out from Railroad Avenue to the east of Washington Street.

Built by Moses Guild to store cargo and wagons, this structure later became a steam-powered factory. In the 1840s, it was converted into tenement housing for early Irish settlers. (Courtesy Norwood Historical Society.)

Initially encountering discrimination and the disdain of some of the town's residents, the Irish kept to themselves and quickly developed a flourishing community of their own with distinctive traditions and activities. They became the mainstay of the Catholic Church, founded in 1863 when the first church building was purchased from the Universalist Society. By 1890, there were approximately 1,500 members of the congregation, still mostly Irish, as St. Catherine of Siena parish obtained its first resident pastor, Reverend James Troy. Troy remained in the post for 17 years, building up a large following and overseeing a rapid expansion of church services. After Father Troy's transfer in 1907, St. Catherine's second pastor, Reverend Thomas McCormack, served the parish for 11 years. It was under his stewardship that the new church, still one of Norwood's architectural landmarks, was built in 1908–1910. Designed by the firm of Maginnis and Walsh, it is an English perpendicular Gothic-style building of gray Roman brick with Indiana limestone trim. Those living in Dublin and Cork City were proud to note that Joseph Conley, John Horgan, and Christopher O'Neil were the first baptisms in the new church on December 25, 1910, and the first marriage in St. Catherine of Siena was that joining Ellen Donovan and Cornelius Cleary on April 17, 1911. The original church building was renamed Columbia Hall and served as a meeting room until its demolition in 1927 to make way for the rectory.

In addition to their dominance of St. Catherine's parish, the Norwood Irish started their own neighborhood stores with Peter Flaherty's grocery store, later known as Shurfine Market, in Dublin. Across the tracks in Cork City,

T.J. Casey's grocery was founded in 1879. In 1890, the firm of Pendergast and Callahan, founded by Edward Pendergast and Daniel Callahan, succeeded Casey and prospered in their store located at 69 Railroad Avenue. Both partners had been born in South Dedham to Irish immigrants. In 1895, John Callahan, Daniel's brother, went into business under the name of the Norwood Furniture Company. A few years later, Daniel joined his brother. Callahan's Norwood Furniture Company occupied 720 Washington Street for decades, rebuilding on the same site after a fire destroyed the store in 1925. According to a publication of the Norwood Business Association, Callahan's offered "practically everything in house-furnishings which could meet the taste or needs of any class of patrons in this town." The business eventually moved to a location on Route 1 in the early 1970s and closed after nearly 100 years of family ownership.

This advertisement celebrates the opening of Pendergast & Callahan, a partnership formed by the sons of immigrants in the Cork City neighborhood.

Another successful Irish American was James Folan who, in 1887, opened a small shoe store at the corner of Washington Street and Railroad Avenue. He increasingly became involved in the town's business community and helped found the Norwood Business Association. Folan's most significant success, however, came in real estate. As a builder of store blocks and multi-family dwellings in South Norwood, he made considerable profit as property values rose dramatically in the early part of the century. Folan was also on the executive committee in charge of the town's handling of the great influenza epidemic of 1918. Folan was joined on this committee by James Pendergast. Son of one of the early steam mill residents, Pendergast had risen to the position of town clerk and accountant in 1911, a job he held until 1939.

Despite these successes, the Irish remained somewhat segregated, and the vast majority remained in the working class. Many Irish found employment at the Lyman Smith's Sons tannery at Railroad Avenue and at the railroad car shops or the American Brake Shoe and Foundry Company. When economic hard times made employment at the local factories uncertain, many Irish shifted to the town's public works, police, and fire departments. By the early decades of the twentieth century, all three were dominated by hard-working sons of Irish immigrants. It was also the Irish who, in the late nineteenth century, led discussions about the rights of workers and unionization at the factories. Casey Hall, built by Thomas Casey behind his store on Railroad Avenue, became the rallying place for members of local trade unions who could not secure a meeting place uptown during their early efforts to organize the town's workingmen.

Taken in the 1890s in front of the Everett School, this photograph of Norwood firefighters demonstrates the shift to public works by the Irish. Pictured are, from left to right, (front row) Keddy, Fulton, Boyden, Robinson, Conley, Welch, Conley, Morgan, O'Brien, and Belcher; and (back row) Tobin, Warner, Dyer, Boyden, and Phalen.

Julius Balduf, a German immigrant and tannery foreman, lived in this Wilson Street home with his family. Several of his children were employed at the tannery. Balduf also ran a bowling alley in a separate building. (Courtesy Ellen MacDonald.)

Casey Hall was also the home of ethnic organizations, including the Ancient Order of Hibernians (AOH). The AOH was a charitable society whose purpose was "to give aid to widows and orphans, to provide for the sick, and to befriend the stranger." The local order, founded by Patrick Spillane, Patrick Walsh, Edward Fay, and Thomas Casey, maintained these principles well into the twentieth century. In 1912, the Norwood Gaelic Club, an organization whose purpose was to promote a United Ireland, pay sick benefits, and perform other beneficial activities for the community, was founded by Patrick Kelly, Daniel Collins, Michael Lydon, and Peter Flaherty. Like the AOH, the Gaelic Club most especially promoted the unity of local Irish Americans. This group continued to meet in the rooms above Clark's Pharmacy in the Conger Block until the 1950s.

Because of the friendship and social supports of these neighborhoods and organizations, the Norwood Irish fostered a chain migration. Family and neighbors from Ireland, particularly from the Gaelic-speaking villages along the South Connemara coast, emigrated not just to America, but to Norwood in particular. Even into the mid-twentieth century, Gaelic was often heard around the neighborhoods and in such local spots as the Irish Heaven, a barroom housed in a small, two-story clapboard building next to the Light Department on Central Street. There, the most accomplished twentieth-century writer of fiction in the Irish language, Máirtín Ó Cadhain, spent many hours. Norwood even figures in Ó Cadhain's 1949 masterpiece work *Cré na Cille*, translated as Churchyard Clay, in which one of the novel's main events is a key character's immigration to Norwood.

At about the same time the Irish were pouring into Guild's steam mill tenement, a number of families arrived from Germany. Two very different businesses, furniture making and tanning, first attracted the more than 30 Germans who arrived between 1850 and 1865. As Willard Everett's furniture company expanded, so did the need for skilled furniture craftsmen and wood carvers. Workers from southern Germany, in particular, sought and obtained these positions and then built homes in northeast Tiot. Originally called "Germantown," this territory became Cork City when the Irish began buying up the property after the Everett factory burned in 1865 and many Germans followed the business to Boston.

A second group of German and Austrian immigrants were attracted to Norwood by the tanneries. Most of these men and their families settled in the southwestern area of Tiot, on and around Wilson Street. Thus was born a new, longer-lived Germantown inhabited by families such as the Eppichs, Baldufs, and Verderbers. Similar to the Irish, these immigrants created a tightly knit community of their own. In 1889, they organized a Turnverein, an athletic club, to promote the health and physical activity of its members. With Vitus Gleichauf as president, in 1893, the group built the Turnhall for its meetings, gymnastics, and German instruction. The Turnverein disbanded in 1908, but the hall remained and in 1915, renamed Winslow Hall, it functioned as a neighborhood civic center in conjunction with

Erected in 1893 as the Turnhall, this structure became headquarters for the International Order of Runeberg Lodge 211 and the Italian-American Lodge 1235 before it was demolished in the late 1990s. (Courtesy International Order of Runeberg, Lodge 211.)

the Norwood Civic Association. In 1927, it became Runeberg Hall when it was purchased by Lodge 211 of the International Order of Runeberg, a Swede-Finn mutual benefit and temperance organization. Runeberg Hall sponsored picnics, musical events, and dances, and also became a favorite site for wedding receptions, birthday parties, and testimonials.

Meanwhile, the Germans moved across Wilson Street and built a second hall, the headquarters of the Workmen's Sick and Dead Benefit Fund. This society was organized sometime between 1895 and 1898, with John Anheiter as its first president, and built Arbeiter Hall in 1901. Membership dues provided assistance to the sick, widowed, or aged in the neighborhood during a time when Social Security did not exist and few businesses offered insurance or medical benefits. Workmen's Hall, as it came to be known, also sponsored festivities and entertainments that filled the area with music, laughter, good food, and camaraderie.

Germantown also had its own healthcare facility, called the Wilson Street Hospital. Around 1900, Mrs. Annie Groote, who lived at 95 Wilson Street, began taking patients into her home. With Dr. Thomas O'Toole as attending physician, the hospital eventually had patient beds, a nursery for newborns, and an operating room. Nurses employed at the hospital boarded in a small house behind Groote's. Shortly after the Norwood Hospital on Washington Street was founded, the Wilson Street facility closed.

A third ethnic enclave sprang up in the areas surrounding Cedar and Chapel Streets and along Savin Avenue. "Swedeville," as it was dubbed, attracted

With the assistance of Dr. Thomas O'Toole, the Wilson Street Hospital, located at 95 Wilson Street, served the Germantown neighborhood during the first two decades of the twentieth century. (Courtesy David Benson.)

The home of Norwood's Swedish Baptists from 1898 to 1902, this small chapel was located on Cedar Street just beyond the railroad tracks into South Norwood. (Courtesy Norwood Historical Society.)

immigrants from both Sweden and Finland beginning in the late nineteenth century. Seeking opportunity and employment, many of the men found work at the tanneries, Bird and Son, and the press complexes, while the women were employed as domestic help in the mansions of the Winslows, Plimptons, Allens, and Morrills. Once again, a number of religious and social associations functioned as social support and traditional folk dances, such as the hambo and schottische, were performed at frequent gatherings held at Runeberg Hall.

For a time after their migration to Norwood, Swedish Baptists, Swedish Congregationalists, and Swedish Lutherans all worshiped together in one of the former Winslow homes at Chapel and Cedar Streets. Within a few years, however, they began to organize into separate parishes where they were often joined by like-minded Germans. In 1898, the Swedish Baptists were incorporated as part of the Swedish Baptist Church of Boston, holding services in a small chapel on Cedar Street. In 1902, with a membership bolstered by a Sunday school, Young People's Society, and Missionary Circle, the congregation moved to a newly built church on Chapel Street, opposite Savin Avenue. The Swedish Baptist Church remained there until the mid-twentieth century when the sanctuary was moved to the corner of Walpole and Berwick Streets. It was remodeled and enlarged and continues today as the Trinity Community Church.

Among the first Swedish settlers in Norwood, Swedish Congregationalists had been members of the First Congregational Church as early as 1889. With the influx of additional Swedes, however, they joined in with the Swedish Baptists and Lutherans. When the Swedish religious groups went their separate ways, the Swedish Congregationalists decided to form their own parish rather than return to the First Congregational community. In June of 1903, a small wooden church, located on the east side of Savin Avenue, was dedicated and a Sunday school and Ladies Sewing Circle were organized. Swedish Congregationalists worshiped there and at a second meetinghouse on Chapel Street, built in 1909, until the church disbanded around 1939.

In 1898, the Swedish Lutherans organized a parish with Carl Johnson, August Peterson, and Axel Carlson among the first officers and trustees. One year later, they dedicated their first church on Cedar Street. They continued to worship there for some 40 years until the present Emmanuel Lutheran Church, designed

Located on Chapel Street, this building was the home of the Swedish Congregational Church from 1909 to 1939. It later became the Church of the Nazarene and the Full Gospel Temple. It was recently converted into a private residence. (Courtesy Norwood Historical Society.)

by local architect Harry J. Korslund, was completed in 1939. A handsome building set at the corner of Berwick Street and Gardner Road, across from the Disabled American Veterans Memorial Park, this church and the Trinity Community Church stand only a short distance from their initial Swedeville locations.

Also inhabiting the Swedeville neighborhood were emigrants from a second Scandinavian country, Finland. Arriving in the 1890s, the Finns quickly established a fairly self-contained enclave that included variety stores, groceries, an auto repair shop, shoemaker, restaurant, and pool hall. Three Finnish institutions—a social hall, a co-operative store, and steam baths—became the centerpieces of the vibrant area. In 1906, as the number of Finns in the community increased, land was purchased on Chapel Court and a small hall was constructed by the Finnish Workingmen's Association. Although some members were decidedly political, causing an ideological split, the main purpose of the organization was to preserve the ethnic identity, customs, and traditions of its members. As its popularity increased, this original hall became inadequate and a new building was erected in 1912. Finnish Hall was constantly busy sponsoring the activities of men's and women's athletic clubs and choirs, a band,

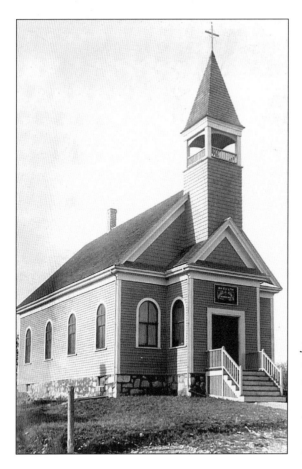

The Swedish Lutheran Church from 1899 until 1939, this building on Cedar Street later became the Italian Christian Church and is currently the home of the Jain Center of Greater Boston. (Courtesy Norwood Historical Society.)

Located on Chapel Court, Finnish Hall was the center of social activity for Norwood's Finns during the early twentieth century. Currently, it is the property of the American Legion Norwood Post No. 70. (Courtesy Aira Koski Johnson.)

drama club, and sewing circle. The hall housed lectures, naturalization classes, religious instruction, and a 1,000-volume library. Young people were encouraged to participate in the theater, music, and athletic programs that enabled them not only to retain the Finnish language but to develop their musical and athletic abilities. In 1959, the building became the property of the American Legion Norwood Post No. 70.

A second Finnish institution, the Co-operative store, first opened its doors at 47 Savin Avenue in 1909, taking over the site vacated by the first Swedish Congregational Church. Originally a branch of the Quincy Co-operative, by 1914, it joined the United Co-operative Society, a loose association of stores situated across Massachusetts. Eventually, this larger organization dissolved and the United Co-operative Society became a stand-alone institution. First utilizing the former church building as best they could, the Co-operative eventually demolished it and erected a two-story structure with space for a dry goods store and later a restaurant, on the second floor. A separate building housed a garage and storage facility. This allowed the store to be well stocked with dry goods, shoes, and other incidentals in addition to the expected meat, groceries, and milk products. The Co-operative also maintained a milk bottling and distribution plant

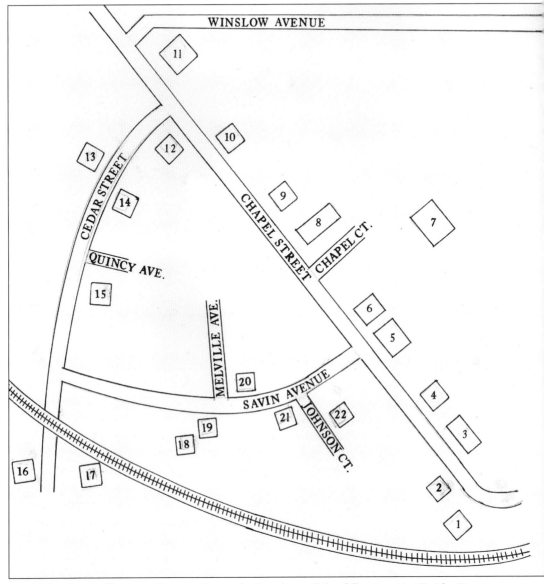

The Swedeville map above indicates the locations of the following: 1. Guido Stuntzner, grocer; 2. George Pratt, barber; 3. numerous businesses; 4. Wilho Maenpaa, grocer; 5. Oscar Bagge, later Olavi "Whitey" Huttunen, grocers, and Andres Kallgren, boots and shoes; 6. Swedish Baptist Church (c. 1902–1954); 7. Finnish Hall; 8. Nickerson Block; 9. George Peterson, express; 10. Swedish Congregational Church (c. 1899–1939); 11. Winslow School; 12. Olavi Huttunen, variety store; 13. Swedish Lutheran Church (c. 1899–1938); 14. G.A. Johnson, grocer; 15. Guido Stuntzner, grocer; 16. Swedish Baptist Church (c. 1898–1902); 17. Kusta Anttila, sauna; 18. August Lehtonen, sauna; 19. Willehead Karki, poolroom; 20. Willehead Karki, candy and variety store, and Kusta Anttila, grocer; 21. Swedish Congregational Church (c. 1903–1909), later United Co-operative Society store; 22. Karl Roth, auto repair.

The United Co-operative Society store was erected on Savin Avenue at the site of the first Swedish Congregational Church building. It was sold in 1953 and is now residential housing. (Courtesy Aira Koski Johnson.)

in North Walpole, where picnic grounds and athletic fields were located as well. Grossing as much as $200,000 in 1920, business declined during the subsequent decades and, after World War II, the milk plant, store, and eventually the society itself were dissolved. The building was sold in 1953.

In addition to the Finnish Hall and the United Co-operative Society, a third enterprise highly valued by the Finns in Swedeville was the steambaths. Decades later, one Norwood resident recalled that "the saunas were a place to meet friends and discuss the events of the day." After a good steaming, thought to cleanse both the body and the spirit, residents would gather for coffee and conversation. Norwood's first public sauna was built by August Lehtonen on Savin Avenue in 1910. A second, larger bathhouse was erected on lower Cedar Street by Kusta Anttila. Subsequently owned by Victor Swami, this sauna was closed in the 1950s and is today a storage garage. The Savin Avenue steambaths finally closed in the 1980s. Next door to the sauna, the last remaining neighborhood landmark, a popular poolroom owned by Willehead Karki at 38 Savin Avenue found continued life, first as a barroom and barbershop, and later as a restaurant. As the Old Colonial Café, the spot became so popular that its telephone number was unlisted. Today, the Old Colonial has moved "uptown" to the former fire station on Nahatan and Central Streets and the Savin Avenue building serves as a function hall.

Eventually, although unofficial social segregation persisted, time and a modest prosperity brought these ethnic groups a certain degree of stability and respectability. At the same time the Irish, German, and Scandinavian natives and their children were beginning to be accepted, however, new immigrants

Extending south on Washington Street from Dean Street, this multi-family dwelling is an example of those that were built in South Norwood during the early twentieth century. Lined up on the sidewalk are gas stores about to be installed. (Courtesy Anne Sansone.)

from Eastern Europe were arriving in large numbers. During the 20-year period between 1890 and 1910, the town's population more than doubled, from 3,732 to 8,014, with foreign-born residents comprising an ever-increasing percentage. This transition to even greater ethnic diversity was not an easy one and problems arose, particularly in South Norwood, in a territory called "The Flats."

The origin of the name "The Flats" is unclear. One version has it that the land itself, located where Tiot's first settlement had been, was once farmland, lower, flatter, and more fertile than the rest of the town. Another states that the term was derived from the many multi-family apartment buildings that arose during the early 1900s, most of them triple deckers with flat roofs. Finally, in a modification of this story, others believe the name came from the term used to identify the apartments themselves; they were called flats, hence the name "The Flats" for that part of town where such dwellings were found in abundance. Geographically, the area was a considerable distance south of what had developed into the commercial center of town near the Hook and, topographically, the Flats were located at the base of a fairly steep hill that dipped underneath a railroad bridge constructed around 1897. As the uptown business district expanded, South Norwood had remained sparsely populated until the manufacturing boom at the turn of the century precipitated the arrival of foreign-born workers. Inexpensive, multi-family dwellings were constructed and, by 1917, more than 200 buildings of this type stood within the confines of South Norwood.

The area quickly became congested and overcrowded and town services, including electricity, sewage, and road paving, were slow to reach South

Norwood. Bryant Tolles, in his centennial history of the town indicated, "This district long remained a shabby, unsanitary, and poorly provided place to live," an area where "the new foreigners had literally been herded together practically as outcasts." Within South Norwood itself, however, the perception was more complex. A vital, ethnically diverse commercial district sprang up to meet the needs of the neighborhood's inhabitants. More than 60 stores of all types, including many multi-lingual establishments, lined the streets. Churches, charitable associations, and clubs provided a wide range of social supports and activities to residents.

One of the first groups to arrive in South Norwood were Lithuanian nationals. According to the memoir of early Lithuanian immigrant Vincas Kudirka, upon his arrival in Norwood in 1902, there were ten Lithuanians living in South Norwood, then still largely undeveloped. He noted the area consisted of about 14 houses, a small schoolhouse, and farmland. The schoolhouse that Kudirka mentioned was the Balch School. Built in 1867 and named after Reverend Thomas Balch, the first pastor of the Congregational Church, the school had replaced the Old Brick (No. 7) schoolhouse as the sole elementary school in the southern precinct. This clapboard-covered building was itself razed to make way for a new Balch School, built in 1913 to serve the ever-increasing number of children in South Norwood.

Similar to other nationalities, the first Lithuanian residents began a chain migration as word spread that jobs and housing were available, and by the state census of 1915, there were over 500 Lithuanian residents in town. Most took low-paying, unskilled jobs primarily in the ink factory, at Bird and Sons, in the tanneries, and the press establishments, all within walking distance of their

This is the second Balch School to be built in South Norwood. Erected in 1913 on the site of the original wooden Balch School, this structure has had several additions and remains a focal point of the neighborhood. (Courtesy Bryant F. Tolles.)

homes and boarding houses. Like the Irish, Germans, and Finns before them, the Lithuanians formed a mutual benefit society to assist their fellow countrymen in times of sickness or death. Within a few years of its inception in 1905, the association, called Kestutis after a famous Lithuanian hero, split apart when Lithuanian freethinkers and socialists gained control and expunged all religious references from the organization's by-laws. By 1913, the religious-minded Catholic Lithuanians had incorporated as the Lithuanian Benefit Society of St. George and members advanced the idea of creating a Roman Catholic parish, separate from St. Catherine of Siena. While the plans for the new church were developed and the funds sought, the diocese granted permission for a weekly liturgy for the Lithuanians to be held in Columbia Hall.

Meanwhile, the Lithuanian freethinkers aimed to build a meeting place that would serve their social, cultural, and educational needs. A rivalry arose between the two factions as each tried to raise its institution first. The freethinkers completed their building on St. George Avenue in November of 1914. The dedication was attended by such local notables as James Hartshorn, George Willett, and Francis O. Winslow, all invoking God, apparently unaware that these particular Lithuanians were non-believers. One year later, in December 1915, the dreams of the Lithuanian churchgoing community were realized when St. George Catholic Church was officially opened on St. James Avenue with Reverend Andrius Daugis as its first resident pastor. Originally intended to be a joint

The former Lithuanian Hall building, erected by Lithuanian freethinkers in 1914, still stands on St. George Avenue today.

St. George Catholic Church was built by Lithuanian immigrants on St. James Avenue in South Norwood. It was officially recognized by the diocese in 1915. (Don McLean photo.)

Lithuanian-Polish parish, for a time services were held at St. George's in both the Lithuanian and Polish languages and members of the St. Peter Polish Society participated in parish events. Within a few years, however, as had happened in other multi-ethnic parishes, the cooperative effort dissolved acrimoniously. By early 1917, Father Daugis had discontinued the separate Mass and catechism classes in Polish and the Poles were no longer supporting St. George's.

Although in some respects culturally similar to the Lithuanians, both having been subsumed within tsarist Russia, the Norwood Poles established a distinctive subculture of their own. Poles lived along different South Norwood streets than Lithuanians, creating separate neighborhoods and unofficial mutual support networks. The Lithuanian and Polish enclaves also played a large part in making South Norwood's business district bustle with commerce. Most Poles shopped at the Polish Co-operative Store at 1057 Washington Street, managed by Charles Prochonowicz in 1924 and, in 1928, by John Uservitch. By the 1920s, most Lithuanians chose between the grocery of B.A. Tumavicus and the South Norwood Market run by Paul Babel. In addition, there was a Lithuanian Co-operative Association grocery at 1108 Washington Street. Lithuanian Kazimieras Grigas opened a cobbler shop, and Frank Shatas set up a photographic studio at 1 St. James Avenue. At the same time, a host of smaller ethnic grocers, and competing barbershops, bakeries, tailors, druggists, and dry goods stores, were all situated within the same ten-block area.

This was one of the many small grocery stores operating in South Norwood during the early part of the twentieth century. Sawdust is sprinkled on the floor. (Courtesy Helen Abdallah Donohue.)

In 1919, 84 members of the Polish community met at the Southern Theatre on Washington Street to discuss the formation of a third Catholic parish within the town's borders. Land and an existing structure on St. Joseph Avenue were purchased and, through the labor and generosity of community members, the building was renovated into St. Peter's. The first official service was held there on Easter Sunday in 1920. Among the founders of St. Peter's Church were Constantine Jankowski, Joseph Adamonis, and John Usewicz. In 1928, the first diocesan priest to be assigned to the parish, Reverend L. A. Ciesinski, arrived. During his six-year tenure, stained-glass windows were added, oak pews installed, the building was painted, and the grounds landscaped. In 1936, a rectory was built next to the church. Throughout that decade and the next, improvements to the physical plant continued with the support of the Polish National Alliance, St. Peter's Men's Society, and St. Peter's Guild. This small but steadfast parish continued to function independently until 1997 when the Archdiocese of Boston closed its doors as part of a parish consolidation program.

The diversity of South Norwood increased further when Syrian Joseph Howard moved his family from Boston sometime in the 1890s. Other members of Boston's Syrian community were attracted by the open space and employment potential of South Norwood as well. In 1903, John Abdallah, owner of a wholesale dry goods store on Kneeland Street in Boston, bought the property then known as the Robbins Estate at the northern end of South

Norwood. Nine years later, Abdallah relocated his family, including his son Nicholas and three-year-old grandson John Alexander Abdallah, to Norwood and opened a general store. South End Hardware, from which the Abdallahs sold household goods, hardware, gardening supplies, dry goods, and toys, became a neighborhood landmark.

Before 1920, approximately 150 Syrians had followed the example of the Howards and the Abdallahs and formed the nucleus of a thriving Lebanese-Syrian enclave. Within the decade, Abraham Kelley, Elias Nassif, and Joseph Eysie each ran grocery stores along Washington Street. In 1918, Joseph Howard organized the St. George Men's Society for the support and betterment of the Syrian community. Charter members included Howard's sons Abdallah and George, as well as Abram Deeb, Sam Boulis, Abraham Assad, Elias Mike, and Ned Kelley. In May of the same year, the Syrian Ladies Society was founded. Now secure in their neighborhood and community, the group next turned their attention to religion. For almost 20 years, residents had traveled to Boston each Sunday to worship, but in 1921, the first Greek Orthodox Catholic Church in Norwood was built. Joseph Howard was once again one of the founders and the Abdallah family donated the church's bell. After a 1933 fire destroyed all but an immense wooden altar crucifix, the parish rebuilt within a year. Erected on the same site on Atwood Avenue as the first church, today's building is a striking asymmetrical Byzantine

St. Peter's Catholic Church, established by Polish immigrants in 1920, was Norwood's third Catholic parish. (Courtesy Hansen and Donahue Collection.)

81

neo-Romanesque structure, unique in the town. The Syrian community maintains a strong presence in South Norwood today, particularly via the Abdallah-owned store that once housed a branch post office and still functions as an unofficial town hall for the neighborhood.

Finally, Italian natives assisted in the diversification of the town beginning in the late nineteenth century. By 1905, there were 28 men and 10 women of Italian birth and 66 of Italian parentage living in Norwood. Many worked in the factories while others tested their entrepreneurial skills. In South Norwood, barbers Iarocce and Poce, shoe cobbler Bruno Bartucca, and grocers Edmando Morini and Salvatore Gulla opened for business in competition with the already existing Polish, Lithuanian, and Syrian establishments. Charles Sansone, Samuel Salemme, and Atilo Balboni each became successful fruit dealers. About a decade later, Danti Balboni was owner of Balboni's Boston and Norwood Express Company. Meanwhile, just north of Swedeville, Torquato Farioli opened a variety store at 68 Walnut Avenue. Farioli's Market remained a popular neighborhood business until the late 1970s when Farioli's sons Peter and Edward sold the family enterprise and retired.

Another Italian family business has been in operation for three generations. In the late 1920s, Umberto Balboni opened a fruit and confectionery store at 860

Shown here in a 1972 photograph, St. George Orthodox Church on Atwood Avenue has remained one of the town's most admired architectural landmarks since 1934. (Courtesy Bryant F. Tolles.)

This South Norwood map includes the following:
1. South End Hardware;
2. St. George Orthodox Church; 3. St. George Catholic Church;
4. Lithuanian Hall;
5. Balch School; 6. St. Peter's Catholic Church.

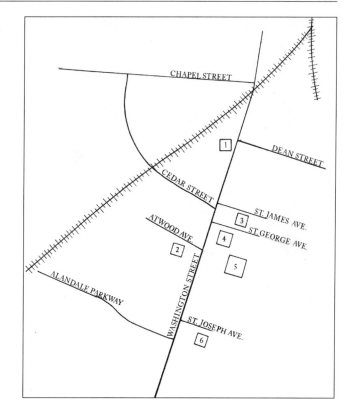

Washington Street in the Hawkins Block. After Prohibition, in 1936, he added beer and wine to his trade. Two years later, the business had become Balboni's Package Store. Balboni was later joined in this enterprise by his son-in-law Donald Bonica. Bonica's own father, Stephen Bonica, had also owned a variety store at 528 Washington Street called the Waiting Room. The location is now Dandy Donuts, a popular morning gathering spot for local residents. In the 1950s, Bonica took over management of Balboni's when Umberto Balboni retired. The store moved to its current location on Washington Street in the 1960s. Today, the store is in the hands of Joan Bonica Lynch, Umberto Balboni's granddaughter and Donald Bonica's daughter.

One particularly well-known Italian American was Anthony B. Sansone. Born in Norwood to Italian immigrant parents, Sansone had a sixth-grade education and then began work in his father's bowling alley in South Norwood. He founded the Norwood Taxi Company in 1919 with Patrick Curran, purchasing two Model-T touring cars used for weddings, funerals, special dates, and hospital transport. By 1937, Sansone had eight cabs and a bus and, a year later, he owned a DeSoto-Plymouth franchise. In 1940, he sold the taxi company to concentrate on the bus service and changed the name to Sansone Motors. At about the same time, he constructed the large white building on Broadway that is still the company's headquarters. Throughout the second half of the century, Tony Sansone worked

This 1940s view of Washington Street, looking north, shows Balboni's on the right in the Hawkins Block. (Courtesy Joan Bonica Lynch.)

tirelessly until his business enterprises included 75 buses, a service station, used car lot, and auto leasing firm. He died in 1996 at the age of 94.

It was not until the 1920s that Italians formed a benefit society, later becoming the Italian American Lodge 1235, affiliated with the Order of Sons of Italy in America Grand Lodge. The association's charter members included Visidoro Ferrara, Domenico Triventi, and Corradino DiBerto. The Norwood Italian Ladies Lodge, an organization devoted to fundraising for worthy causes, was founded in 1933. In the late twentieth century, the Lodge purchased Runeberg Hall from the International Order of Runeberg, but, lacking the income to sustain it, sold the property for development. In 1949, another group of Norwood residents established the Italian Social Club "to unite all people of Italian descent, to encourage Italian culture, to assist social welfare, and to organize institutions of charity." Chiefly a neighborhood association, this group sponsors numerous social and charitable events.

In the 1930s, a group of Italian Americans, reportedly dissatisfied with their treatment at the Irish-dominated St. Catherine of Siena, founded the Assemblia Cristiano, or Italian Christian Church. For the first seven years or so, their Italian Protestant Pentecostal services were conducted at various locations in South Norwood. When the Emmanuel Lutherans moved to their new sanctuary on Berwick Street in 1939, the Italian Christian Church was formally incorporated and purchased the Lutheran property on Cedar Street. Thirty years later, having become more ethnically diverse, they changed their name to the Christian Church of Norwood. In 1977, the church relocated to a new site on Walpole Street, becoming the Living Waters Church.

The dissatisfaction that caused some Italians to withdraw from St. Catherine of Siena parish was a familiar feeling to many living in South Norwood. Several older residents who grew up in the neighborhood recall vividly the sting of prejudice. "We were looked at as substandard, although the uptowners will never admit to that," recounted one Syrian gentleman. An elderly Italian resident recollected that the uptowners "always thought of this as the slums." Other residents remember that even their names seemed unimportant. One Lithuanian man reported "the people at the town hall didn't want the people to have a foreign name, they'd spell them any which way." Another told of a grade school teacher who "standardized" their names. Even the usage of the term "The Flats" in reference to the district indicated a certain level of disdain as it was often used in a derogatory manner.

Three incidents stand out as demonstrations of the deep, if unconscious, institutional prejudice that existed: a police scandal, the town's World War I preparedness campaign, and an influenza epidemic. The first occurred in 1913 when Chief of Police James W. Lavers was charged with extortion and influence peddling. A public hearing was held on 21 charges, all involving immigrants from South Norwood. Salvatore Gulla, Paul Babel, Tekla Oaglish, John Zurba, Adolph Utorto, and many others had paid money to the chief, upon his demand, either to influence police action or to obtain permission to serve liquor or hold social functions. Most of the witnesses required interpreters because they could not read or write English. When called to the stand, Chief Lavers, who had been chief of police since 1909, generally denied all charges, but offered little in the way of a defense. Before the board of selectmen could render a decision, Lavers resigned.

Norwood Taxi was founded in 1919 by Anthony Sansone and Patrick Curran. Their service was used for weddings, funerals, and special occasions, as well as early school transportation. (Courtesy Anne Sansone.)

Although the police hearing raised public awareness of inequitable treatment in South Norwood, the rest of Norwood continued to view activity in the area as if it were a foreign country. According to a 1916 *Norwood Messenger* article, "a great number of people have never visited this section of town," an indication both of how rapidly the neighborhood had developed and how isolated its residents were. The newspaper also added to the uptown community's uneasiness regarding South Norwood with numerous reports of raids, civil disturbances, and violence. People living in South Norwood felt the ostracism. They had been limited to the least expensive housing by their economic situation. Factory workers lived in boardinghouses and many families shared housing to offset costs. They had few contacts with members of other groups and even less with American-born residents. This mutual segregation and distrust came to a head with the onset of World War I.

In the months prior to the United States' entrance into the conflict, a huge public relations campaign to make war a palatable option and to generate support for the British and hatred for the Germans took place. Irish Americans who had been anti-British during the Irish Easter Rebellion of 1916 were forced to hide or deny these sentiments as pro-British propaganda was disseminated to the American people. In addition, all things German were demonized.

In March of 1917, Norwood held a preparedness parade and organized its own General Committee for Public Safety. The purpose of this committee was

Arbeiter Hall on Wilson Street was built by German immigrants in 1901. When anti-German sentiments ran high with the onset of World War I, the mutual benefit association changed the hall's name to Workmen's Hall to demonstrate their allegiance to the United States. This original building was destroyed by fire in 1955. (Courtesy Workmen's Hall, Inc.)

to coordinate and promote war-related drilling squads, food and clothing drives, and informational committees. One subcommittee of the General Committee for Public Safety was known as the Night Riders. Every night, young men, sworn in as special police and armed, patrolled the town in automobiles "to guard against possible sabotage to public and industrial property." Once war was declared in April of 1917, anti-German harassment became common practice. Dr. Hugo Riemer, a government service physician living in Norwood, protested the treatment he had received at the hands of town officials. One German American recalled feeling "like a skunk at a lawn party," while another remembered finding a basket of rocks on her doorstep on May Day in 1917.

As in other communities, this anti-German bias quickly included all foreign nationals and anti-German sentiments were transformed into more general anti-radical and anti-socialist fears. This last presented a considerable problem in Norwood where there was a fairly large socialist contingent. Socialist and radical politicians had often made the town a stop on their lecture tours. In December of 1916, a socialist speaker drew a crowd of 500 and in July of 1917, an outdoor socialist rally was attended by 300. When socialists boycotted the town's Patriot's Day rally in 1917 and then celebrated May Day at Lithuanian Hall, suspicions were heightened. The local police and visiting United States marshals observed the well-attended services to ensure that no anti-American statements were made. When the United States entered the war in Europe, the situation worsened as immigrants were accused of being "alien slackers" and un-American, further polarizing the community and isolating the immigrants.

In truth, Norwood had nothing to fear from its foreign-born population. The town's response to the national crisis reflected the patriotism of all its inhabitants. After the declaration of war, a massive demonstration, parade, and rally of 3,000 residents included hundreds of foreign nationals. Ethnic organizations joined with other civic groups to raise funds, sell Liberty Bonds, and participate in Red Cross work. In June of 1917, the registration of all males between the ages of 21 and 30 was held at Everett Hall in the Civic and the first group of draftees left for Camp Devens in September. By the end of the war, over 600 Norwood men had served in the American military and 13 were killed in the line of duty. Several of these were immigrants or the children of immigrants.

Norwood lost nearly seven times this many in the influenza epidemic of 1918, an occurrence that, in some respects, opened the community's eyes to the divisions that had grown up between residents and neighborhoods. The 1918 pandemic was no trifling matter. It was responsible for more deaths, 20 to 30 million worldwide, in a shorter period of time, than any epidemic in history. The United States alone lost close to 750,000 residents within a year. Norwood was especially hard hit for a town its size, losing nearly 100 people. As illness spread rapidly through the town in October of 1918, an emergency hospital was established at the Civic association building, schools and theaters were closed, and all church services and public meetings were cancelled. Still, Norwood's response to the disease reflected ingrained attitudes and fears.

Once it became apparent that Norwood's foreign-born laborers were dying, the official response was quick and sharp. While middle- and upper-class residents were allowed home visits by local physicians, immigrant neighborhoods were canvassed and searched, and the sick were transported to the emergency hospital, often against their will. Once at the Civic, the patients were denied visitors and placed on army cots, where they received minimal attention because the volunteer staff was overwhelmed by the number of victims. Displaying a lack of understanding of the infectious nature of the disease, an airborne virus easily spread in crowded environments, newspaper reports suggested that unsanitary living conditions, deficient personal hygiene, and lack of assimilation were the causes of the epidemic. As a consequence, uncertainty and fear increased, and many immigrant families, fearing deportation, failed to report cases of illness and even deaths. When the epidemic episode subsided in late October, statistics showed that just under 78 percent of the deaths had been foreign-born adults or underage children of immigrant parentage. Over half of the deaths occurred in South Norwood. The ethnic populations hit the hardest were recorded as Russian (which included Poles and Lithuanians), Italians, and Irish.

If any good came of the experience, however, it was the awakening of concern on the part of community leaders and American-born citizens. In the words of town historian W.W. Everett, the epidemic tragedy caused many people to look at South Norwood in a new light. "They realized for the first time that it could no longer be ignored as a real-estate speculator's paradise and the dumping ground of the peasantry of Europe." The suffering and deaths of so many residents forced the town to recognize South Norwood as an integral part of the larger community and to address the needs of the neighborhood.

A few years later, the 1920 census showed that the town's population had risen to 12,627, a nearly 60 percent increase in ten years. As Norwood prepared for its 50th anniversary, there was reason to celebrate. The world was at peace, industries in town were flourishing, and modernization measures were progressing. While the pains of immigration had not been solved, there was a heightened recognition of the problems of diversity and the community was attempting to be more inclusive. At the gala jubilee festivities held in October 1922, Irish, Swedish, and Italian dancing was highlighted and representatives from the Italian-American Society, the Ancient Order of Hibernians, Workmen's Hall, the Lithuanian Citizen's Club, the Hebrew Congregation, the Syrian and Swedish Churches, and many more organizations, were all part of the pageant. In addition, the program itself listed a representative sampling of 131 residents of foreign birth or descent from 14 nationalities to demonstrate renewed fellowship within the community. Norwood had undergone a dramatic transformation in its first 50 years. At this significant juncture, the town was looking to George F. Willett and Frank G. Allen, two men who had emerged as civic, business, and political leaders, to steer the community into the future.

5. THE WILLETT-ALLEN ERA

By the turn of the twentieth century, Norwood was no different from a dozen other manufacturing towns in Massachusetts; it too had grown in a haphazard fashion without the benefit of an all-encompassing plan for the future. But that was about to change with the arrival of two talented men, George F. Willett and Frank G. Allen.

George Willett was a driven man, and his philanthropic vision for Norwood was very nearly matched by his business genius and a pragmatic ability to get things done. Frank Allen was an astute businessman and politician, rising from working class to industrialist and from Norwood's board of assessors to governor of the Commonwealth. During the years 1900 to 1940, these two men, who married the daughters of tannery owner Francis O. Winslow, were largely responsible for turning Norwood from a small, backwater town with a few successful industries into a modern, cohesive, forward-thinking community. Their personal relationship, however, founded on professional compatibility and familial bonds, dissolved into rancor and distrust. While their achievements were monumental, their lives were the stuff of legend. Both deserve closer examination.

Born on August 7, 1870 in Walpole, Massachusetts, where his ancestors had settled some 200 years before, George Willett grew to have, as one historian put it, "a greater impact upon the development of the town of Norwood than any other individual in the course of its history." He spent his early life in Walpole, attended public schools, and later studied industrial chemistry at Boston University. He entered the wool business in Boston and, along with partner Edmund H. Sears, formed a holding company that operated a chain of various industries for the manufacture of carpets, shoes, felt, and other related products. Willett quickly amassed a fortune and Willett, Sears and Company became known for the successful reorganization and management of industrial concerns.

In 1893, Willett married Edith Winslow, daughter of F.O. Winslow, part owner of the Winslow Brothers tannery. A former state representative and president of the Norwood Co-operative Bank, Winslow was a true gentleman, courtly in his bearing, devoted to the growth of the community, and generous to all civic causes. The last surviving original town official, Winslow was often called upon to recount events surrounding the community's origins. Four years before his death, he delivered the historical address at Norwood's 50th anniversary celebration in 1922.

Following his marriage to Winslow's daughter, Willett built a home near his in-laws and became involved in the operation of the tannery. By 1895, at the age of 25, he acquired controlling interest in Winslow Brothers where he replaced age-old practices, such as tasting the liquor in the tanning vats to see if it was chemically correct, with modern scientific methods of operation and quality control. Two years later, he purchased the second family-owned tannery in town, Lyman Smith's Sons. There he installed wool pulling and scouring facilities and, with these and other advanced practices, both tanneries increased profits dramatically. In 1901, he merged the two firms into Winslow Brothers and Smith, thereby reconsolidating what George Winslow and Lyman Smith had divided in 1853 and bringing Norwood's tannery history full circle.

By 1909, still not 40 years old, Willett, through ingenuity, keen business instincts, and intelligence, had parlayed his modest beginnings into a burgeoning

This oil painting of George F. Willett hangs in the Willett Room of the World War II Memorial Civic Center on Nahatan Street. Willett had "a greater impact upon the development of the town of Norwood than any other individual in the course of its history."

George Willett's shingle-style turn of the century home, situated on Walpole Street next to F.O. Winslow's mansion, was demolished to make way for a modern elder care facility. (Courtesy Norwood Historical Society.)

empire. He had made millions and his own income was approaching $500,000 annually. With his financial fortune established, Willett felt it was time to give back to his adopted community. Years later, he recalled his intentions: "From that time on my chief aim was to try to do something to justify my existence. I felt grateful, I wanted to do something for humanity, for my fellow-man, and to do the right thing." He turned his genius and his inexhaustible energy to this avocation and his scrutiny could not have come at a better time. Norwood had the highest property tax rate in the state ($25.60 per thousand) yet, despite this, the town had no public buildings other than wooden and ill-repaired schoolhouses, no recreational areas, no all-inclusive civic organizations or healthcare facilities. In effect, the town's social and civic conditions had lagged behind its manufacturing advances.

Under Willett's voluntary guidance, within the next decade Norwood saw extensive civic improvements. As a direct result of his intervention, properties were reexamined and reassessed, lowering the tax rate to a mere $8.50 per thousand, and budgetary controls were put in place. The question of implementing sound business practices within town government was addressed and ultimately led to a new town charter, approved by voters in 1914. Spearheaded by Willett and other reformers, Norwood became the first town in New England and only the 12th in the country to adopt the town manager form of government, placing the day-to-day business of the community in the hands of a management professional. Willett's plans for Norwood went far beyond municipal reform, however, and ultimately resulted in a civic association, a housing association, a hospital, the revamping of the entire downtown business district, and his one unfinished dream: Westover.

The Norwood Civic Association was in many respects the linchpin of Willett's vision. To his mind, the most important task before the town was the creation of community spirit and dedication through a civic organization. Purchasing a large segment of land near the center of town, formerly the site of the Willard Everett furniture factory, Willett constructed a clubhouse containing an auditorium, gymnasium, swimming pool, billiard room, bowling alley, social hall, and individual meeting rooms. The grounds provided recreational playing fields and tennis courts. Gymnasium classes were offered with trained instructors; lectures and entertainment programs were scheduled; exhibitions and contests were held; and instruction in English, citizenship, and homemaking was encouraged. "The Civic," as it was known, offered athletic programs, health services, vocational training, and social service assistance to all residents of the town for a $1 per year membership. Willett's efforts earned him a glowing endorsement from the *Boston Globe* Sunday Magazine on June 29, 1913. In a lengthy, much illustrated article, Willett was deemed a "visionary," and was congratulated for his recognition of the widening class divide in Norwood and his work to eliminate corresponding social problems.

George Willett was unquestionably a Progressive and, as such, believed scientific principles and business strategies could solve social ills; he also sought to indoctrinate immigrants into the American way of life. In light of this philosophy, the Civic was a Progressive institution, whose purpose was, as W.W. Everett put it, "to teach the newly-arrived foreign peoples the lessons of love and respect for America, the existence of neighborliness among the Yanks, the lesson of cleanliness and sanitation, the value of education, and the usefulness of healthy recreation and athletics." To that end, the association's monthly publication, *The*

This view of the buildings of the Norwood Civic Association was taken at the height of its popularity. The running track is visible in the foreground. (Courtesy Hansen and Donahue Collection.)

Civic Herald, also trumpeted the benefits of assimilation and offered solutions to "the immigrant problem." While many resented the paternalistic undertones of Willett's Civic, and some young immigrants stayed away, preferring to join programs offered at Finnish or Lithuanian Halls, the institution was eventually embraced. By the 1920s, it had become the social, cultural, and, to some extent, educational center of the community.

Willett himself put over $500,000 into the Civic buildings. After the facility was extensively damaged by fires in 1924 and 1930, he sold the nearly ruined property to the town, which continued many of its programs in subsequent decades and even enhanced the center's offerings. In 1952, for example, Norwood was one of the first communities in the state to provide services for its elder citizens. Over the years, this program too has expanded and today the Norwood Senior Center, housed in an addition to the former Junior High North, serves a large number of senior residents. In 1969, the town constructed an addition to the Recreation Department buildings, the World War II Memorial Community Center. Its new gymnasium became the scene of men's basketball and volleyball, youth floor hockey leagues, women's indoor tennis lessons, and baton and marching practice for young girls. The addition also contained weightlifting equipment and a sauna bath. The swimming pool in the older building continued to be open seven days a week and offered swimming lessons, water ballet, Red Cross water safety instruction, and family swims, as well as sponsoring a competitive swim team known as the Norwood Sting Rays. The Recreation Department also sponsored summer activities at 14 playgrounds throughout the town. By 1970,

The World War II Memorial Community Center was added to the recreation department complex in 1969. The entire facility was sold to the Norwood Hospital corporation and razed in the early 1980s. (Courtesy Bryant F. Tolles.)

The Norwood Trust Company was established by George Willett to assist in the financing of his development plans. It was located at the former site of the Joseph Day house at the corner of Day and Washington Streets. (Courtesy Hansen and Donahue Collection.)

"Tot Lots," recreational areas designed for younger children, were springing up at many locations. In 1981, the Recreation Department buildings and grounds on Washington Street were sold to the Norwood Hospital and demolished to make way for a hospital wing. Today, the Recreation Department is headquartered in the former State Armory building on Nahatan Street and still maintains a wide range of programs for people of all ages.

Perhaps the most important and unique feature of the civic association was the manner in which it was to be funded. Willett proposed the Civic be financed through a second community-oriented organization, the Norwood Housing Association. He formed the housing association to hold both unimproved land in the outlying districts and improved properties in the residential and business sections of town. Some land could be sold for factory sites so that the industrial development of the community could continue and jobs would be available; other property would be retained for recreation. Willett also planned to build multiple houses using standardized methods of construction and materials to minimize costs. According to Willett, he planned "to build, in wholesale fashion, say 10 to 20 houses at a time, to obtain the lowest possible costs. Yet each house was to have its own design and distinctive individuality so as to gain the most attractive results for the neighborhood." In addition, the Housing Association controlled the 5 miles of shore of nearby Willett Pond, a man-made body of water formed to power the tannery. Willett named the pond not for himself, but for his ancestors who had lived near its shores in Walpole. To local residents, it remains "New Pond." Willett proposed that the housing association build bathhouses, boathouses, and recreational facilities as well as summer bungalows on the shores of the water. Under his direction, the income from all this construction and development would generate an endowment fund for the civic association. He projected that the Civic would have sufficient income from this source to meet all its budgetary needs within a few years.

To ensure the success of his plans, Willett established a bank, the Norwood Trust Company. He was the first president of the bank and selected the institution's first board of directors himself. The Norwood Trust Company was to assist in the planning and financing of the construction of, not only homes, but also substantial business blocks in the downtown area. Willett also secured a charter for a Morris Plan Bank to handle small loans. In this way, he stated, "it was planned to cover the entire financial requirements of the community, so that any man with a good character and a good job could own a good home." The town of Norwood was to become an example of what sound management could provide for a community in terms of security, employment, recreational and educational services, and even home-building and buying power.

Another aspect of Willett's vision of Norwood concerned healthcare. At the time, the Wilson Street Hospital and a private facility run by Dr. Eben C. Norton in his home on Washington Street were the only facilities for the care of the sick in the town. Already outdated by the early twentieth century, Norton's "hospital" was purchased by Willett in 1913. At his direction, a two-family residence called the "Old Corner House," which he had purchased along with land for the civic association buildings, was moved from East Hoyle Street to a site adjacent to the

*The first Norwood Hospital consisted of the former home of Dr. Eben C. Norton and a structure known as the Old Corner House. It stood near the site of the current post office building. (*The Civic Herald, *November 1917.)*

Norton house. There, a health center consisting of a 23-bed hospital, an operating room, a dental clinic, and an eye clinic was formed. The building was also the headquarters for the board of relief as well as district nurses then delivering home care in the area. The little hospital was almost immediately in great demand and, five years later, proved vastly inadequate for the emergency generated by the influenza epidemic of 1918 when the civic association building itself was opened to care for the overflow of patients.

In December of 1918, a group of concerned citizens, including Herbert M. Plimpton, Walter F. Tilton, James A. Hartshorn, Francis J. Foley, Alfred N. Ambrose, and R. Russell Williamson, formed the Norwood Hospital Corporation. In March 1919, the corporation took title to the facility Willett had organized and almost immediately made plans to build a modern hospital with 85 beds and a nursery unit of 15 bassinets. This structure was completed in 1926 and two years later, thanks to the generosity of Herbert Plimpton, who served as the president of the hospital's board of trustees for 25 years, an administration building was annexed to the plant. The Depression of the 1930s slowed progress, but the following two decades resulted in rapid expansion. In 1942, a new "south" wing was added to the main hospital building and the maternity and pediatric departments were enhanced. Six years later, a new laundry, power plant, and more in-patient wards were added. In 1952, 50 new beds, enlarged laboratory facilities, and modern operating rooms were made possible by a two-story addition to the "east" wing.

This aerial view of the Norwood Hospital captures the original brick hospital and several of the early to mid-twentieth century additions. (Courtesy Hansen and Donahue Collection.)

This combination Norwood Junior/Senior High School building was opened in 1919. Two years later, a wing was added. (Courtesy Hansen and Donahue Collection.)

Sensing an ever-increasing need for services during the post–World War II population boom, the Norwood Hospital next engaged in a fundraising drive that resulted in the expansion project of the early 1960s. Once completed, the three-story "west" wing contained 110 additional patient beds, an administrative area, a recovery room, and new x-ray, pharmacy, and emergency departments. In 1981, after protracted debate and negotiation, the hospital purchased the remaining Civic property on Washington Street.

The creation and expansion of the hospital's physical plant was not the only modernization project that Willett helped to initiate, however. From 1912 until 1923, he served as chairman of the town's planning board, the committee entrusted with the oversight of Norwood's physical development. During that time, Willett planned and implemented a drastic alteration and refurbishment of the town center. The Hook disappeared as Willett bought and moved the aging Village Hall and Tiot Tavern buildings. Market Street, or Cemetery Way as it was formerly known, with its ragtag assemblage of wooden shacks and stores, was wiped from the map. Central Street was then extended parallel to Washington Street. This new configuration created the current town square and municipal building lots, as well as additional tracts, later filled by a row of storefronts and the Norwood Theatre, erected in 1927.

Meanwhile, on the west side of Washington Street the former homes of Joseph Day, Joel Baker, Lyman Smith, and L.W. Bigelow, the pride of the village in the mid-nineteenth century, were turned and moved back onto Day, Vernon, and Cottage Streets to make way for new commercial business blocks.

Due to overcrowding at the Washington Street school, this impressive senior high building on Nichols Street was constructed in 1926. (Courtesy Hansen and Donahue Collection.)

Farther south on Washington Street, a new combination junior and senior high school building was opened in 1919. The town's original high school, built in 1889 and situated on Beacon Street behind the Morrill Memorial Library, became an elementary school and was renamed the Beacon School. Within two years, the new high school was overcrowded and a wing, opened in 1921, eased the problem for only three more years. In 1926, this building was converted into the town's junior high building when the Norwood Senior High School, a sprawling, red-brick neo-Federal building with clock tower, was completed. At George Willett's suggestion, the school was located on Nichols Street, some distance from the town's commercial district and, after additions in 1931 and 1962, remains an impressive complex. Interestingly, the land for the senior high school was given to the town by George F. Willett and Frank G. Allen at a time when their own long-standing co-operative relationship was at its lowest point.

When people in Norwood think of Frank Allen, it is often in tandem with George Willett, for the events of the first few decades of the twentieth century inextricably linked these two remarkable men. Born in 1874 in Lynn, Massachusetts to working-class parents, Frank Allen graduated from Lynn Classical High School and passed the Harvard College entrance examination, but lacked the funds to enroll. Instead, he went directly to work as a gauge watcher in a small leather factory in Lynn and soon decided that the industry would be his career. At the age of 22, he was employed at Winslow Brothers tannery where his initiative, intelligence, and innate talent ensured his success. One year after his arrival in Norwood, in 1897, he married Clara Winslow, the elder daughter of Francis O. Winslow, becoming brother-in-law by marriage to George Willett. The two shared a belief in the application of business practices to governmental institutions. On more than one occasion, Allen remarked that he was "a plain businessman trying to use business methods in carrying on the State's affairs." For his part, Willett lectured across the country advocating the same philosophy, even publishing his ideas in a 1915 pamphlet entitled "Can Business Methods be Applied to the Conduct of Municipal Affairs?" With such a shared outlook, the two men worked well together and Allen became a close, trusted advisor to George Willett. Allen entered the executive offices within the tannery, eventually rising to the positions of president and chairman of the board.

Allen began his political career in Norwood as well, serving as chairman of the board of assessors from 1911 until 1915. When the new town charter was approved and implemented, Allen was elected to the board of selectmen from 1915 to 1924. In 1918 and 1919, following in his father-in-law's footsteps, he was a member of the Massachusetts House of Representatives where he was particularly active on taxation and financial issues and the Special Commission on Street Railways. His term in the House was followed by election to the Massachusetts State Senate in 1920. The following year, he was selected by his peers to be president of the State Senate, a position he held for four years. Allen was elected to two terms as lieutenant governor in 1924 and 1926 and won the praise of then Governor Fuller, who stated that "No man has ever served under the gilded dome of the State House with more fidelity, integrity, and painstaking attention to this State's business." In 1928, as the Republican Party's nominee, Frank G. Allen was elected governor of the Commonwealth of Massachusetts and served one term. As governor, he was known for his honest dealing, his reduction of the debt, and a public welfare program inaugurated to aid handicapped children. He was also one of the first to recognize an impending economic crisis and created the Massachusetts Emergency Commission on Unemployment.

With the Depression gaining momentum after the stock market crash of 1929, and the popularity of the Democratic Party rising, Allen was defeated in his bid for reelection in 1930 by Joseph B. Ely. Upon his defeat, Allen retired from public office and returned to a rigorous schedule as chairman of the board of directors at Winslow Brothers and Smith Company. He also held several other trustee and directorship positions with Atlantic Mutual Indemnity Company, Boston Chamber of Commerce, Boston University, Boston & Providence Railroad Company, John Hancock Mutual Life Insurance Company, and others. He continued to serve the local community as a director of the Norwood Co-operative Bank and trustee of the Norwood Hospital despite the long shadow cast by the events surrounding the collapse of George Willett's empire.

In 1917, with his industrial holdings in excellent condition and his municipal ventures progressing, Willett was invited by the Wilson administration to aid in the war effort. He traveled to Washington, D.C. along with many of his top executives, turning his financial affairs over to a few trusted advisors, bankers, and consultants, among them Frank G. Allen. During his absence, Willett's

Frank G. Allen was inaugurated governor of the Commonwealth of Massachusetts in January of 1929. He served one term. (Courtesy Norwood Historical Society.)

business ventures took a turn for the worse and an attempt to put together a package of loans to stabilize his holdings failed. As a result, he was forced to sell a substantial portion of his portfolio for a fraction of its value. After consideration, however, Willett concluded that the handling of the matter by his bankers and financial consultants had been fraudulent, aimed solely at gaining control of his business. In that light, he and his partner, Edmund H. Sears, brought suit against those involved. Eventually, Sears dropped out of the proceedings, leaving Willett the sole plaintiff in a case that rocked the Boston financial community to its foundation. Defendants in the suit consisted of a who's who in Boston banking and finance, including Robert F. Herrick, counsel for the First National Bank; Daniel G. Wing, president of the First National Bank; F.S. Mosely and Company; and Kidder, Peabody and Company. It was Willett's contention that these men had conspired to take his fortune from him by blocking normal financial options, thereby causing a cash crisis that, in turn, made the value of his holdings appear questionable.

The trial was history making. It began on November 5, 1923 and ended on December 18, 1924. Its length, 184 court days, made it the longest running civil trial in history; Willett himself testified for 45 days. The trial transcript filled more than 30 volumes, some 16,300 pages. During the year, a special act of the state legislature was passed to increase each juror's pay to $9 a day, but it was still a hardship for many. One juror had a nervous breakdown and special permission was obtained to complete the trial with less than a full complement of jurors. As might be imagined, Willett became even more of a local folk hero as the town of Norwood saw its greatest benefactor fighting fiercely in the toughest battle he would ever enter. Finally the verdict was returned. *Norwood Messenger* newsboys called out the decision in December 1924, that the jury had found in Willett's favor and had awarded him more than $10 million. In an almost unbelievable twist, the paper also revealed that Willett himself lay suffering from typhoid fever in his Norwood home. Less than 24 hours before the verdict was read, he had been close to death.

Willett recovered his health, but his hard-won victory was short lived. The Massachusetts Supreme Judicial Court set aside the decision of the Superior Court jury. It was the higher court's view that a general release, signed by both Willett and Sears, protecting their financial advisors from legal actions, was valid. It had been Willett's contention that the release was part of the alleged conspiracy, that those who encouraged him to sign the release had misrepresented themselves and profited from the results. The decision brought a moving reaction from both the townspeople and the local newspaper. Commenting on the Supreme Court's 1927 reversal of the lower court decision, a local editorial remarked:

> the majority of Norwood's residents, native and newcomer, will feel a big surge of sympathy for George Willett, who has done much to advance the welfare of this, his adopted home town. He is a fighter of remarkable tenacity, whose fight for civic growth, civic beauty, and civic planning, has had the heart of the people with it all the time. In this hard buffet of fate, he will have the backing of every Norwood man and woman, and our earnest appreciation of what he has done for Norwood.

The United States Supreme Court refused to hear the case, thereby allowing Willett's defeat to stand.

While all this was going on, Frank Allen was making a steady rise to the State's highest office and the town was reaping the benefits of the achievements of both men. The Civic was becoming an institution, the hospital was expanding, the junior/senior high school was enlarged, and a new senior high school was opened. And in the late 1920s came the completion of the "Million Dollar Town Square," as the plans first envisioned by George Willett slowly came to fruition with the help of Frank Allen. In May of 1926, after a delay of several years, town meeting members voted an appropriation to construct the Municipal Building as a memorial to Norwood residents who had served in World War I. Ground was broken in August of 1927 for the striking neo-Gothic, cathedral-like edifice and tower many believe represents the best work ever achieved by its architect, William G. Upham. Inspired by buildings at Princeton University, Upham and the E.F. Minor Building Company used Weymouth seamed-face granite to fashion the structure.

The November 11, 1928 dedication ceremony, held on the tenth anniversary of the end of the war, was attended by some 10,000 people. There were parades, speeches, and the official dedication of the structure "built to commemorate the patriotism and valor of the men and women from Norwood who served our country in time of war." Many of Norwood's most prominent residents made meaningful contributions to the building. The window in the Memorial Chapel was donated by Frank G. Allen, then lieutenant governor; the memorial tablets were provided by Charles J. Prescott; and the names of the war veterans going back to the Colonial conflicts were compiled by F. Holland Day. Following the ceremony, those in attendance heard the first carillon concert presented on a magnificent 51-bell instrument housed in the building's soaring tower. Cast by the English bell and clock makers Gillett and Johnston, the largest bell is 71 inches in diameter and the smallest is 6 1/2 inches. The initial concert by noted Belgian carillonneur Kamiel LeFevre was broadcast live over Boston radio station WEEI.

The Norwood Memorial Municipal Building, with its striking tower, and St. Catherine of Siena Church on the opposite corner, make an impressive pairing in this 1972 photograph. (Courtesy Bryant F. Tolles.)

The State Armory, dedicated in 1930, was designed to complement the existing Municipal Building, which stands a block to the west. (Courtesy Hansen and Donahue Collection.)

Donated to the town by Walter F. Tilton, the president of the Norwood Trust Company, the carillon quickly became the pride of the community.

In January 1930, dedication ceremonies for the State Armory on Nahatan Street were held. This project had been some five years in the making with then governor Frank Allen breaking ground in June 1929, only five months after his inauguration. The armory is constructed in a style complementary to the Municipal Building, which stands a block to the west. The structure served the town well in subsequent decades, housing Massachusetts National Guard units, serving as an auditorium and voting place for residents, and, most recently, as the home of the Norwood Recreation Department.

As Frank Allen wielded the power and garnered the praise for his success in politics, George Willett continued to be frustrated in his efforts to complete the capstone to his plans for Norwood, a residential complex called Westover. Intended to be a model for other communities to follow, Westover was to be, in Willett's words, "a Garden Village of the Twentieth Century" with hundreds of individualized, distinctive homes set in a carefully designed 1,000-acre undeveloped area in Norwood and part of Westwood. This was not to be a residential community for the wealthy, however, but "for the family of ordinary means who appreciated simple, tasteful architecture, and pleasant natural surroundings." Although some land was set aside for large estates, the majority of house lots were modest in size. The complex was to feature a system of one-way, tree-lined parkways, integrated open-space recreational areas, a golf course, and opportunity for fishing and swimming in adjacent Willett Pond. Even after the court defeat, George Willett had managed to salvage Westover and remnants of the Norwood Housing Association, which owned much of the Westover property.

Frustrated by continual delays in the project and still angered by the outcome of the Willett-Sears case, Willett became obsessive and paranoid, and his private suspicions spilled out into public accusations. On March 24, 1930, at an otherwise routine town meeting, Willett took the floor, blamed "forces invisible" for the delay of his Westover development, and implored town meeting members to back his visionary plan. Restrained by the town moderator James Halloran, who refused to allow him to digress into personalities, Willett called his own private "town meeting" in the Civic's Everett Hall on April 8. In front of a capacity crowd with hundreds more turned away, Willett gave a rambling two-hour account of his entire career and financial demise. In a stunning development, for the first time, Willett publicly identified Frank Allen as his chief adversary, charging him with a betrayal of trust and labeling him the culprit behind the loss of his fortune. Frank Allen, then governor of the Commonwealth, denied the charges. Although nothing ever came of Willett's indictment, the accusations reverberated for decades within the town.

Never giving up on Westover, Willett built two model homes and received federal assistance during the Depression to construct some of the proposed streets. To many residents, these came to be known as the "Crazy Roads," paved asphalt leading nowhere. By the 1950s, in personal bankruptcy, Willett still continued to appear before town committees and at town meetings in a vain

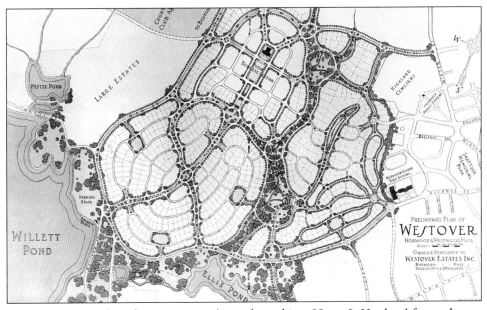

This preliminary plan of Westover was drawn by architect Harry J. Korslund from a layout by George Willett and was included in Willett's proposal, Westover: A New England Village of the Twentieth Century, *c. 1934.*

St. Timothy's Roman Catholic Church was constructed in the 1960s on a beautiful site overlooking Willett Pond. (Courtesy Bryant F. Tolles.)

attempt to salvage his "garden village." In 1952, he was declared incompetent and placed under the guardianship of his children, Francis and Martha. One year later, in 1953, he was forced to declare the Westover Corporation in bankruptcy. Outside business interests purchased the property and began erecting "Westover" as it now exists. A few years later, the Town of Norwood, disputing Willett's claim that he was operating New Pond as a charity, took him to court for non-payment of taxes and won, but refused to buy the pond for $35,000. The Archdiocese of Boston purchased the land overlooking Willett Pond, which had come to be considered the town's recreational beach, and established St. Timothy's Roman Catholic Church in 1963. The congregation was made up of parishioners from St. Catherine of Siena in Norwood, the Blessed Sacrament Church in Walpole, and St. Margaret Mary's Church in Westwood.

As for Frank G. Allen, he too remained an active participant in Norwood affairs for several years following his political defeat. Shortly after their 1897 marriage, Allen and his wife Clara Winslow had built a substantial shingle-style house on Fisher Street, just north of his Winslow in-laws' property, Oak View. In 1913, the Allens and their daughter Mary moved into the Winslow mansion at 289 Walpole Street, next door to Willett's home. In 1924, Clara Winslow Allen died after a lengthy illness and, three years later, Frank Allen, then lieutenant governor, married Eleanor Hamilton Wallace, who was a Wellesley College classmate of his daughter Mary. In 1929, Allen hired William Upham, the Municipal Building's architect, to make extensive renovations to the mansion, including the enclosure of the northern piazza as a conservatory. The couple and their family remained in the house during his term as governor and throughout the personally turbulent times brought on by Willett's accusations.

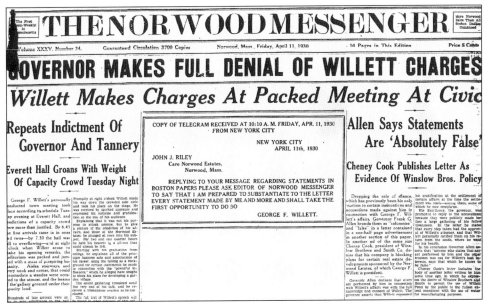

The Norwood Messenger *covered George Willett's accusatory speech and Governor Allen's denial in its April 11, 1930 issue.*

Under the presidency of Frank G. Allen, Winslow Brothers and Smith tannery was merged with the Eastern Leather Company, a subsidiary of the J.K. Mossett Leather Corporation. During the summer of 1933, workers at the tannery joined the National Leather Workers Association. After a violent strike in December of that year, which pit state and local police against the workers and their sympathizers, the union was recognized and a wage agreement was reached. By the late 1930s, the tannery had fallen on hard times caused by, as one observer noted, "a diminishing demand for its products, rising operational costs, the expense of raw materials, and labor problems." In 1938, another particularly rancorous strike, during which Allen's home was damaged by labor supporters, nearly crippled the enterprise.

In 1944, Frank Allen, still chairman of the board of directors of the tannery, ended his 48-year residence in Norwood, moving to Boston's Back Bay, and the Missionary Servants of the Most Blessed Trinity took over the Oak View property. Locally referred to as "The Cenacle," the mansion remained the home of the religious order until 1977. Today, it is a private residence and, since 1989, the site of the Oak View Museum of Dollhouses. Despite his relocation, Allen continued to give generously to worthwhile Norwood projects. In 1947, he personally donated $4,500 to the Norwood Hospital Building Fund and was instrumental in Winslow Brothers and Smith's $20,000 corporate contribution. In 1949, another strike interfered with business at the tannery and the enterprise commenced its departure from the town by closing down the Railroad Avenue facility. In December of that year, Allen retired as chairman of the board and, in

October 1950, at the age of 76, he died at his Boston home. A little more than a year later, in January 1952, the remaining Winslow Brothers and Smith plant in Norwood was closed.

George Willett, meanwhile, had moved from Norwood after his wife's death to the Country Club in Brookline where he spent most of his last 20 years. He died in 1962 at the age of 91. Six years later, the Town of Norwood built the George F. Willett Elementary School, situated on Westover Parkway, on land Willett had tried so desperately to develop. A few decades later, the building became the school department's administration offices. In 2002, school authorities approved moving the administrative functions to the former Junior High North, converting the Willett into a system-wide kindergarten facility. Willett's Walpole Street mansion was renovated into a nursing home and, subsequently, razed to make way for a more modern facility called Charlwell House.

George F. Willett and Frank G. Allen were, at various times, friends, relatives, business partners, and enemies. The two stand as towering figures when one considers the political, industrial, and civic development of Norwood in the early twentieth century. Very few, if any, lasting institutions do not owe a debt to their foresight, fortitude, and financial assistance. Still united by these good works, both men returned to Norwood after their deaths and are memorialized a few yards from one another in Highland Cemetery.

The extensive renovations made to the Winslow mansion in 1929 by Frank Allen can be seen in this 1997 photograph of the home. (Courtesy Barbara J. Rand and Robert Pegurri.)

6. Business and Politics

The Depression of the 1930s, World War II, and the post-war era collectively caused many communities across the country to undergo significant change. Privately-owned businesses and industrial entrepreneurs gave way to corporate conglomerates while the blue-collar work force declined in the face of a dramatic expansion of the middle class. In addition, the very definition of middle class shifted. In the late nineteenth and early twentieth centuries, the middle class had been composed of self-employed small business owners and independent professionals such as physicians and lawyers. By the mid-twentieth century, however, the expanding middle class was predominantly made up of salaried employees working in corporate or government bureaucracies. Similarly, towns like Norwood that had once been nearly self-contained places where people lived, worked, and shopped, were being transformed into residential-industrial suburbs, virtual bedroom communities providing housing for the increasing number of bureaucratic employees. The story of the decades extending roughly from 1930 to 1970, then, is one of transition, as Norwood struggled to maintain its character and retain its bearings in the light of a nearly total industrial, residential, and municipal reconfiguration.

Because of the dominance of a few major industries, the Depression of the 1930s hit Norwood particularly hard. A reallocation of town funds, combined with federal relief assistance, brought temporary work to the unemployed and enabled some municipal projects to move forward. In 1934, U.S. Route 1, the Providence Highway, was completed, offering hope for future development. Upon its completion, plans were implemented to extend Nahatan Street from the center of town to the new turnpike. A neo-Gothic bridge was designed by William Upham to allow Nahatan Street traffic to pass beneath the railroad tracks east of the town square. The structure was completed in July of 1935 and the town was connected via East Cross Street to the new highway. It was not until midway through 1958 that Nahatan Street was extended through to the Providence Highway and the now familiar cloverleaf was officially opened.

Although there was no widespread economic recovery for Norwood until World War II, when military needs revived local manufacturing and 2,230 young people went off in defense of the nation, these decades did bring an economic shift. The large-scale industries, that had come to be relied on, disappeared and were replaced by a variety of light manufacturers, laboratories, and wholesale businesses. Labor unrest affected Eastern Leather Company, the owners of Winslow Brothers and Smith, with strikes in 1933, 1938, and again in 1949. After the last disturbance, the Railroad Avenue facility was closed, followed three years later by the closure of the Endicott Street operation. The latter buildings were occupied by several businesses while the Railroad Avenue structures were demolished. The early 1950s also brought the demise of the Norwood Press. After World War II, the conglomerate experienced operating deficits and a gradual decline in production. In April of 1952, following a labor-management deadlock, the plants began to close. Berwick and Smith Company was dissolved in October of 1952 followed by C.B. Fleming and Company and J.S. Cushing and Company in 1954.

George H. Morrill Company and the Plimpton Press managed to continue until the early 1970s. Morrill's had existed as a family business until 1929 when it merged with four other manufacturers as the General Printing Ink Company. The conglomerate gradually scaled back its Norwood facility, known as the Sun Chemical Corporation. In 1972, the final Norwood division moved to Mansfield, Massachusetts. Meanwhile, beginning in 1955, the controlling interest in the Plimpton Press passed through various investors and corporations until its Norwood facility was closed in the early 1970s, bringing an unprecedented era of industry and growth to an end.

This view shows the Veterans Road housing that was erected for veterans and their families shortly after World War II. It was replaced by the Washington Heights development. (Courtesy Hansen and Donahue Collection.)

Stepping into the void left by these industrial giants were numerous business ventures beginning with Bendix-Marine in 1942. Manufacturers of navigation control instruments for the U.S. Navy, this enterprise, a division of Bendix Aviation Corporation, established a factory at the intersection of Dean Street and the newly developed Providence Highway. Although it remained in Norwood for only four years, the factory provided a temporary stimulus to the local economy. From 1943 to 1945, it became the town's largest employer, hiring close to 1,300 to meet its government contract deadlines during the war. Demand for its products quickly diminished after the Allied victory and the plant was sold to Tobe Deutschmann Corporation in 1947. During the next few decades, the facility became the property of Cornell-Dubilier Electronics Corporation, a firm that, like Deutschmann's, produced filters, capacitors, and other electrical equipment, and the Kelex Company, manufacturers of electrical power distribution equipment. Following an Environmental Protection Agency mandated clean up of PCBs in the early 1980s, the site now serves as an automobile storage area.

Also in 1942, south of the Bendix plant on Route 1, Factory Mutual opened a research division. A mutual property insurance company, FM Global, as it is known today, focuses on loss control and prevention. It insures the assets of manufacturers, service providers, and government and educational institutions of all sizes and types. The company works with customers to safeguard their property by combining cost-effective insurance with customized engineering solutions designed to reduce overall risk.

The Savogran Company, manufacturers of household and industrial cleaning compounds, opened a plant on Lenox Street in 1947. Founded in 1875 as the India Alkali Works, the company was housed in the historic India Wharf building in Boston. It changed its name to Savogran in 1926 and, two decades later, moved its production line to Norwood. Taking up residence in part of the former railroad car shops, the facility proved so efficient that, within a year, the remainder of the Boston manufacturing division was installed in Norwood. Today, Savogran is an employee-owned company producing a variety of retail and industrial removers, cleaners, and patching materials.

The decades of the 1950s and 1960s brought several additional enterprises to Norwood, helping to rebuild the town's industrial base. In 1952, a producer of gyroscope and accelerometer components, known first as Detroit Controls and then Control Engineering, moved into a one-story brick building between Providence Highway and Access Road. In 1960, Control Engineering was acquired by Northrop Corporation, then one of the country's leading designers of aircraft, aerospace, and military equipment. Integrated into Northrop's worldwide operations as the Precision Products Department, the Norwood facility built inertial sensors, and gyros and gyro systems for the space and defense programs. By the early 1970s, Northrop was utilizing the former Norwood Press building on Washington Street as well as a large property on Morse Street for research and development laboratories and production facilities.

Another enterprise with close ties to government development work, Masoneilan International, Inc., arrived in Norwood in 1956 at the intersection of Nahatan Street and Route 1. Founded originally in 1882 as the Mason Regulator Company, it was named after one of its founders, William B. Mason, a steam engineer and inventor. By the early twentieth century, the company was manufacturing a variety of air, water, and steam regulating valves and combination regulators, and provided a large quantity of control equipment to the U.S. Navy during World War I. Subsequently, in an effort to expand its product line, Mason purchased the Neilan Company of California and, in 1931, became Mason-Neilan Regulator Company. During World War II, Mason-Neilan built a variety of special controls for naval and maritime operations. By the 1950s, the company's Dorchester, Massachusetts site was deemed inadequate and a modern complex was constructed in Norwood. After a series of buyouts, mergers, and name changes, the enterprise became Masoneilan International, Inc.

The town's post–World War II economic surge continued with the arrival, in 1960, of the Raytheon Data Systems Company, a subsidiary of the internationally known Raytheon Company. By the early 1970s, executive offices and a manufacturing complex were located at a Providence Highway site and a smaller building off Dean Street housed purchasing and storage facilities. Like Northrop and Masoneilan International, Raytheon's groundbreaking research and design engineering for data systems resulted in a number of government contracts. Providing employment opportunities for highly skilled engineers and technical workers, Raytheon rapidly became a significant industrial concern.

Norwood's economy received a further boost in 1963 when New London Mills, Inc., a floor covering company, moved its operations into town from New London, Connecticut, having acquired the South Norwood plant of Bird and Son, Inc. Six years later, in 1969, the Connecticut facility was closed and all administrative, manufacturing, and storage functions were brought to Norwood.

In 1964, a 130-acre tract of land, encompassing University Avenue, Canton Street, and American Drive, was designated as the Norwood Research and Industrial Park and began to attract both manufacturing and business interests. Finally, in 1967, Polaroid Corporation's arrival in the Forbes Estate mansion and surrounding property completed the near total shift from printing, tanning, and ink making to light manufacturing, electronics, data systems, and control equipment.

Smaller, more specialized, enterprises contributed to the rejuvenation of industrial and commercial Norwood as well. For example, Peters and Sons Manufacturing, a family business founded in Newton in 1911, arrived at the old tannery complex on Endicott Street in 1959 and made service award pins and ceremonial keys for towns and cities from that location until the 1980s. C.A. Briggs Company, a family business that produced HB Hospital Brand cough drops, built a factory on Endicott Street in 1962. Ten years later, the company sold its product line to Y&S Candies who, in turn, became part of Hershey. The factory was closed in 1976. And finally, Edward H. Allen Company, an outgrowth of the Boston Piano Supply Company that occupied Village Hall in 1916, produced felt piano dampers in a small one-room wooden factory on Walpole Street from 1955 until 1980 when the company was relocated to Mexico.

As more manufacturing enterprises were attracted to town, the labor force began to increase as well. Between the years 1930 and 1970, Norwood's population more than doubled, from 15,059 to 30,815, necessitating new residential areas and options. Developments blossomed along the roads that expanded out from Neponset, Pleasant, Dean, Union, and Sumner Streets. Further hastened by the construction of Providence Highway in the 1930s, and Interstate 95 in the 1960s, this area was extremely popular among families seeking housing within easy commuting distance to Boston or the industrial complexes sprouting up along Route 128. As the twentieth century progressed, these territories continued to expand with new developments of large, well-appointed homes going up between the two highways off the Sumner-Union intersection and beside Neponset Street, overlooking Route 95.

On the opposite side of town, across from the Highland Cemetery, George Willett's Norwood Housing Association offered house lots in a development to be called "Everett Heights." Known locally today as "the tree streets," including Elm, Cypress, Sycamore, and Spruce, the neighborhood contains substantial, attractive homes on modest lots along comfortable, shaded streets. A few years later, following the bankruptcy of Willett's corporation, the Westover properties were developed by outside interests on the wooded area known by some as Germany Plains.

Residential expansion of another sort was the result of a 1948 Massachusetts state law guaranteeing low-cost housing to war veterans. The Norwood Housing Authority was formed within a matter of weeks and, by the end of the year, plans were underway to construct a million-dollar veteran's housing project on land northeast of Roosevelt Avenue. The development, known as "Washington Heights," was dedicated in December 1950. It replaced the temporary Veterans Road barracks that had been erected immediately after the war off Winter Street between Bellevue Avenue and the cemetery.

With veterans' housing being realized, the town next turned to provide for its senior citizens. In 1959, through the auspices of the Norwood Housing Authority, land at the intersection of Adams Street and Railroad Avenue, was designated for the construction of Norwood's first senior housing complex. By 1968, another senior citizen development was erected on southwest Nahatan Street and, in the mid-1980s, two more elderly complexes were added, one on Brookview Circle, off Everett Street, and the other at William Shyne Circle, utilizing the former Shattuck Elementary School and surrounding property. Federal law also allows 13.5 percent of these units to be distributed to disabled and handicapped persons. Today, at all of these locations, the Norwood Housing Authority owns 75 two- and three-bedroom units within the Washington Heights development and 406 one-bedroom units within the four elderly complexes.

By the mid-1960s, due to zoning restrictions and the scarcity of land, Norwood entered the apartment age in its quest for continued expansion. Since that time,

This monument commemorates the Washington Heights development for veterans, built under the auspices of the Norwood Housing Authority. (Don McLean photo.)

developments of what have been called "garden-type units" have predominated. The first and largest of these is Windsor Gardens. Built on a 28-acre tract on Walpole Street, just north of the Walpole town line, the initial units were completed in 1964. Situated within a series of irregular courtyards to provide residents with the optimum of privacy, the complex also contained recreational facilities, laundry and storage areas, and a commuter train station. Within a few years, several townhouse buildings were added and today, Windsor Gardens contains approximately 914 one-, two-, and three-bedroom apartments and townhouse units. Several less ambitious apartment complexes were developed in the ensuing decades with Fisher Gardens in 1969, Norwest Woods in the early 1970s, Norwood Gardens in the mid-1970s, and Olde Derby Village in the mid-1980s being the largest.

Allowing for growth at a time when land was becoming scarce, these apartment complexes also played a part in Norwood's changing demographics. By the late 1960s, many new residents commuted to Boston or highway points north or south for employment, introducing the idea of a "bedroom community" to the town. In addition, an increasing number of commercial concerns were being operated by non-residents, and properties, particularly those where apartments such as Windsor Gardens and Norwest Woods were erected, were being purchased by absentee owners. While all of this changed the dynamic of the community in certain ways, the municipal life of the town remained responsive to its residents and their needs.

113

First of all, the 1930s began with much discussion about the location for a new post office building. Postal service had been established in South Dedham in 1846 when Moses Guild became the first postmaster; the office itself was located at Jabez Boyden's general store, at the site of the present-day United Church. By the time of Norwood's incorporation in 1872, the post office was situated in Village Hall, but in succeeding decades, the operation moved several times, to the Wheelock Building, the Bigelow Block, the Talbot Building, and the Norwood Associates Block. Eventually, townspeople decided it was time to erect a permanent post office. After considerable debate, it was agreed to build on the Everett School site at the junction of Central, Washington, and Guild Streets. Subsequently, a handsome neo-Federal style building, designed by William Upham, was constructed and dedicated in 1934. At the same time, Central Street was extended through the former schoolyard, thereby creating the Aaron Guild Park. For a time, South Norwood had its own post office, located first in Abdallah's store on Washington Street. Later, following the repeal of Prohibition and the licensing of the sale of liquor in Nick's Package Store, the post office was relocated to the Balch Pharmacy. It was eventually consolidated into the main operation at Central Street. Enlarged in 1965, the post office continues to serve the entire community.

In the late 1940s, the town's electorate approved the adoption of a representative town meeting government, which provided for the creation of districts (today there are nine) within the town, from which representatives are elected to attend scheduled town meetings. This was a modern modification of the traditional, and sometimes unwieldy, New England town meeting where any qualified voter

This neo-Federal style post office, located on Central Street, was designed by William Upham and dedicated in 1934. (Courtesy Hansen and Donahue Collection.)

could attend and participate. As Norwood's residential districts expanded, this change was a logical one that ensured more balanced representation for a diverse citizenry with varying issues and concerns.

Norwood's school system also underwent a series of changes during this time period. In 1926, St. Catherine of Siena School was established on Nahatan Street by then pastor Father James Doherty. During its first years, the small grade school provided instruction to 63 children. An addition to the school building was erected in 1931, followed by a second building with an auditorium in 1952, and a third structure in 1960. Today, the school provides pre-kindergarten through eighth grade instruction to some 670 students.

There was also considerable reconfiguration and expansion of the public elementary schools. In 1923, the Balch School received an eight-room addition; but, six years later, the Guild was destroyed by fire and, at about the same time, the Beacon, East, and Everett Schools were taken out of service. The Cornelius M. Callahan School, named for a former school committee chairman, was constructed. This school, along with the Balch, Shattuck, Winslow, and the two-room West School, met the needs of Norwood's elementary school pupils until the population explosion of the post-war years began to take its toll. In 1958 and 1959, two new elementary schools, the Charles J. Prescott School and the Frederick A. Cleveland School, identical in exterior appearance and interior layout, were constructed. Each was situated within the new residential districts that had grown up in the preceding decade. The Prescott School, named after a former chairman of the Norwood Finance Commission, was located across Route 1, off Richland Road, while the Cleveland, named for a former school committee member and noted educator, was built near the Westover development. Expansion continued into the next decade when the John P. Oldham Elementary School, named after a former supervisor of custodians, buildings, and grounds for the school department, was completed; additions to the Cleveland and Balch Schools were made; and the George F. Willett Elementary School was erected in 1968.

On the secondary level, the senior high on Nichols Street and the junior high on Washington Street efficiently handled the town's secondary school population for more than 40 years. In 1968, the Junior High North was opened and the Washington Street building became Junior High South. Less than three years later, in January of 1971, this latter school was nearly lost to fire. The following year, town meeting members voted to replace the school with a new Junior High South to be built on Washington Street in South Norwood and the damaged junior high was converted into the Aaron Guild Elementary School.

Another important addition to the town's educational system was the opening of the Henry O. Peabody School for Girls. This institution was the result of a long and arduous process. The Henry O. Peabody Trust, which included funds for the construction and endowment of a girls' vocational school, was initially established in 1903 by Henry O. Peabody. Peabody had inherited a fortune from the production of firearms during the Civil War, but the trust remained unused for

The Henry O. Peabody School for Girls was built adjacent to the Norwood Senior High School in 1942. The school closed in 1989 and its rooms were integrated into the senior high complex. (Courtesy Bryant F. Tolles.)

decades until 1936 when the town agreed to erect a suitable building. Housed in an edifice connected to the senior high and designed to complement the existing structure, the Henry O. Peabody School for Girls opened in September of 1942. Eventually the school offered co-educational and adult programs in business, food trade, beauty culture, practical nursing, art, and occupational training. In 1989, the Henry O. Peabody School was closed and its curriculum absorbed into the Blue Hills Regional Technical High School located in Canton, Massachusetts. The Henry O. Peabody School's classrooms were integrated into the Norwood Senior High School complex.

The town's fire and police departments and facilities were also modernized, beginning with the evolution of the firefighting force from a principally volunteer organization to a company of professional firefighters, and the addition of ambulance and rescue services to the department's duties. The unit also played a significant part in the establishment of the town's civil defense organization.

Throughout this time period, the dedicated corps of firefighters was also faced with some of the worst conflagrations in their history. In 1925, the Norwood Furniture Company, owned by Daniel and John Callahan, was destroyed by a fire that took hours to bring under control and threatened the surrounding commercial buildings. Close to 10,000 people witnessed the large plate-glass windows blow out and the extensive store inventory go up in a smoky blaze. Five years later, the Norwood Civic Association suffered a nearly total loss when the facility was engulfed in a massive blaze that threatened the nearby hospital buildings. When it was over, only a small section of the civic complex was left standing. It was the Civic's second fire in six years and after this incident, George Willett sold the Civic to the town.

In this same era, the Guild School was lost to a huge blaze and the Guild Theatre was heavily damaged, as were Fales' Railroad Avenue grain mill and the Norwood Lumber Company. These last two fires burned for days on the hay and feed at Fales' and the stock and sheds of the lumber company. Another hazard plaguing firefighters was the reoccurrence of smoldering fires in the peat along the Neponset River. Burning underground and fed by the boggy meadow grass, these fires defied all efforts to extinguish them. They would sometimes burn indefinitely, making the ground hot under foot, and sending up clouds of pungent, thick smoke.

In 1955, Workmen's Hall on Wilson Street went up in flames and had to be rebuilt; in 1962, Roll-Land, a popular roller-skating rink on Providence Highway, was destroyed; and in 1970, Sansone Motor's garage and automobile dealership on Broadway suffered some $200,000 in damage. Two of the town's most significant structures were fully involved in devastating fires in 1964 and 1971. Village Hall, one of Norwood's most historic landmarks, caught fire at the corner of Nahatan Street and Broadway just as it was being prepared for demolition in 1964. Seven years later, the Junior High South, once the town's combined junior/senior high school, lost a significant portion of its physical plant in a spectacular January arson fire. Aided by departments from a dozen neighboring communities, but hampered by the darkness, snow, and freezing temperatures, firefighters were fortunate to salvage as much of the structure as they did.

After nearly 60 years on the corner of Nahatan and Central Streets, a new fire and police station, located farther east on Nahatan Street, was dedicated in 1964. Designed by the local firm of Korslund, LeNormand and Quann, Inc. and erected on an area known as Dunn's Pond, formerly a favorite ice skating spot, the modern brick structure remained the home of these two departments until the end of the century. The police and fire departments were moved to temporary headquarters while the 1964 building was demolished and a new three-story facility, equipped to house both departments well into the future, is being erected. There will also be room at the new station for the Norwood Firefighters Memorial Bell. Placed on a monument setting built by firefighters themselves and dedicated in 1969, the bell has an even longer history. Cast in 1833 in Millis, Massachusetts, by Holbrook and Sons foundry, the bell was first placed on America No. 10, later called Norwood No. 2, the fire station at the intersection of Washington and Chapel Streets. It was then moved to the fire station on Market Street, which later became the temporary town hall. In 1928, when this structure was torn down and the Norwood Memorial Municipal Building was built, the bell was put into storage at the Ellis pumping station. Some 41 years later, it was refurbished by the town's firefighters and placed as a permanent memorial to departed comrades.

Beginning in 1896, the Norwood Police Department, once an informal constable system, became a professional department. Always keeping pace with modern law enforcement educational trends, techniques, and requirements, the department has grown steadily since that time. For many years, the unit worked out of the town offices or shared space with the fire department in the Central Street facility, while prisoners were held in the old lock-up on Market Street, now Central. Detention cells were relocated to the Nahatan Street building when the force joined the fire department there in 1964. The police are currently housed in temporary quarters on Access Road and will return to the new police/fire station on Nahatan when it is completed.

Another municipal department that managed to keep pace with mid-twentieth century change was the library. Since its presentation to the town in 1898, the Morrill Memorial Library has had two additions and a major renovation. In 1928, a three-story wing was added to the rear of the granite Romanesque building as a result of a bequest from the estate of Alice Morrill Plimpton, the sister of Sara Bond Morrill. The second expansion was completed in 1966. Designed by the firm of Korslund, LeNormand, and Quann, the front entrance was moved forward and two new wings were added, greatly increasing reading room and stack space. The use of Norridgewock granite on both these additions preserved the building's distinctive exterior.

As the end of the twentieth century approached, age, along with dramatic technological advancements, dictated that the library undergo an extensive interior renovation to upgrade the building and meet the needs of the community.

This police and fire station building, erected in 1964 on the site of the former Dunn's Pond, was demolished in 2001 to make way for a new three-story facility. (Courtesy Norwood Historical Society.)

This memorial bell is dedicated to all Norwood firefighters. The bell was used originally in the town's first fire station and was reconditioned by members of the department in the 1960s. (Courtesy Norwood Historical Society.)

Completed in 2001, the project, designed by CBT/Childs Bertman Tseckares, updated the heating, cooling, and technological infrastructure and provided maximum utilization of existing space. At the same time, the new interior design unifies the original 1898 building with its more recent additions while preserving and restoring woodwork, stained-glass windows, and the Plimpton wing rotunda in a successful marriage of preservation and modern technology.

At the same time, the Morrill Memorial Library has always tried to offer the best possible services to its constituency. In 1921, the Children's Room was opened and children's story-reading hours became a virtual institution. With the Plimpton wing addition, an Intermediate Reading Room was established and, in 1934, the Young Adults Room was built into the attic of the rear ell. During the 1940s, under then director Edna Phillips, the library instituted a circulating library at the Norwood Hospital, a library-school collaboration, and a branch library in South Norwood.

The branch was opened at the request of neighborhood residents and the South Norwood Merchants Association, a group founded to improve town services within the district. In addition to the storefront library, organized efforts resulted in street lighting, road repairs, designated recreation areas, the Hawes Pool, and the Cedar Street bridge, an improvement long in coming. From the outset, the South Norwood branch library proved a popular venue for residents of South Norwood, Morse Hill, and the new developments off Dean, Union, and Sumner Streets. In 1971, a new 5,000-volume South Norwood branch, located at the Eysie complex farther south on Washington Street, was dedicated. Five years later, due to rising costs and a duplication of services, the South Norwood branch was closed.

The library, and the South Norwood branch in particular, was also the site of one of the most painful and politically charged episodes of the 1950s. Early in

The 1966 addition to the Morrill Memorial Library moved the front entrance forward, adding badly needed space while retaining the building's distinctive exterior and roof lines. (Courtesy Bryant F. Tolles.)

the decade, under the leadership of Senator Joseph McCarthy of Wisconsin, an ongoing investigation into the role of Communists in government and in other areas of American life was conducted. At the same time, the Senate Internal Security Subcommittee, under Senator William F. Jenner of Indiana, investigated Communism in education. In 1953, the Jenner Committee subpoenaed Mrs. Mary Knowles, a five-year employee of the Morrill Memorial Library and the South Norwood branch librarian. Knowles had been identified as a Communist by FBI informant and counterspy Herbert Philbrick. He had purportedly known her in 1947 while she was employed as a secretary at the Samuel Adams School for Social Studies in Boston. Pending the receipt of further information, library trustees suspended Knowles after a four-hour meeting during which she told trustees that she was unaware the Adams School had been a communist front institution. The meeting drew considerable press coverage, requiring a police presence and, when Knowles attempted to leave the building, the police had to step in to prevent a possible melee.

In front of the Jenner Committee, Knowles declined to answer all inquiries, neither confirming nor denying her membership in the Communist Party, and issued only a brief statement that she believed "attempts to impose conformity of thought or religion by using the weapons of economic pressure and unwanted publicity . . . is a deep threat to our liberties and to the strength of the United States." Following pressure from the Daughters of the American Revolution, who demanded her dismissal, and the Community Chest, which threatened to cut off financial support to the library, Knowles was fired. Making a political statement of their own, junior high classmates of Knowles's son Jonathan promptly voted him president of his class.

Mary Knowles was hired by the Jeanes Library, a Quaker organization, of Plymouth Meeting, Pennsylvania, which later received a $5,000 award from the Ford Foundation's Fund for the Republic for "courageous and effective defense of democratic principles" in refusing to give in to pressure to dismiss her. In November 1956, Knowles was indicted by a federal grand jury for contempt of Congress and, two months later, she was convicted and sentenced to 120 days in jail and a fine of $500. In June of 1960, the Court of Appeals for the District of Columbia reversed her conviction and dismissed the indictment.

The Knowles case was not South Norwood's first encounter with governmental extremism, however, as three decades earlier, just after World War I, the district had been part of the infamous Palmer Raids. Then attorney general of the United States, A. Mitchell Palmer, fearing the activities of dangerous radicals throughout the country, organized a General Intelligence Division, the forerunner of the Federal Bureau of Investigation. Under the division's 24-year-old director J. Edgar Hoover, agents infiltrated labor unions and ethnic associations and issued press releases to feed the public's anti-immigrant bias. During 1919, a spate of

The South Norwood branch of the Morrill Memorial Library occupied this storefront beginning in 1941. (Courtesy Morrill Memorial Library.)

bombings directed at business leaders and high government officials, including Palmer, took place. Although no proof was ever offered connecting these incendiary devices to any specific group, Hoover and Palmer made the most of the incidents.

On January 2, 1920, police departments and justice department officials participated in synchronized night raids across 23 states, arresting between 2,000 and 3,000 alleged radicals, most without warrants or probable cause affidavits. The majority of the raids took place in private homes, restaurants, and social clubs. Literature, club membership lists, books, papers, and even pictures on the wall were taken as evidence, also without search warrants. Norwood was one of Palmer's targeted communities. With its large contingent of foreign-born residents, most living in the concentrated area of South Norwood, it was an ideal location for Palmer's raiders. The chief of police, several patrolmen, and two justice department agents carried out the raids. Ten men were arrested on January 2 and two others were picked up the following week. One man was apprehended in Lithuanian Hall, one in nearby Millis, and the rest in their own homes in South Norwood. The *Norwood Messenger* reported that all were seized "on suspicion of being Reds or members of the Communist Party." In almost every case, the authorities contended that they had found "large quantities of revolutionary and Communist literature in the men's homes."

All the Massachusetts victims of these raids were marched through the streets of Boston in chains, taken to Deer Island for processing, crowded into jail cells, held incommunicado, and deprived of their right to counsel. Enraged, the assistant secretary of labor, calling the entire episode "a gigantic and cruel hoax," stated that most of the individuals seized were "perfectly quiet and harmless working people." Courts across the country recognized that the Department of Justice had violated the constitutional rights of the men. The raids also failed to prove that the so-called radicals were bent on violence. Despite the elaborate surveillance and planning that went into the operation, only three revolvers and no explosives were found during any of the nationwide raids. Ultimately, the majority of those seized in the Palmer raids were released and, by 1921, at least four of the men arrested in Norwood had returned to the community where they took up their "perfectly quiet and harmless working" lives.

Still, despite occasional political upheaval, overall the community continued to be a tolerant one, characterized by an ecumenical spirit. And, from 1930 through 1970, there was considerable activity among religious groups, beginning with the 1934 merger of the Universalist and the Methodist Churches. Together, they became the United Church of Norwood. The Universalists had roots going back to 1827 when a small group of parishioners of the First Congregational Church broke away to form their own, more liberal, congregation. The Methodist Episcopal Church was officially organized in 1887 after 13 years of informal gatherings. A small wooden chapel was built on Day Street the following year and the parish remained there until 1900 when a new shingle and stone church was built at the junction of Walpole and Washington Streets. Here the Methodist

The Methodist Episcopal Church, erected in 1900 at Walpole and Washington Streets, became the First Church of Christ, Scientist in 1934 after the Methodists merged with the Universalist congregation to form the United Church. (Courtesy Norwood Historical Society.)

Episcopal Church remained until 1933 when the Universalist and Methodist Episcopal parishioners came to believe they could best serve the spiritual and religious interests of their respective communities through a union of numbers and resources. Joint services were held for a trial period at the end of which the United Church came into existence on June 5, 1934. Since its inception, the United Church has used the sanctuary and parish facilities of the former Universalist Church.

The former Methodist Episcopal Church building was almost immediately rented by the First Church of Christ, Scientist. Originally organized in 1920 as a branch of the First Church of Christ, Scientist in Boston, the society had met in a number of locations until the Methodist Church building became available. In 1938, they were formally incorporated and the Reading Room, still located in downtown Norwood, was opened. In 1940, the property of the former Methodist Episcopal Church was purchased. Since that time, extensive renovations, expansions, and landscaping have been completed, and the church continues to serve the community at large through its Reading Room and the sponsorship of public lectures.

The first mission services of the Episcopal Church were held in Norwood in 1890 and sporadically after that until 1904 when a canvas of the town found

This beautiful stucco and half-timber church stood at 1 Walpole Street and was the home of the Episcopal congregation from 1910 until 1962. (Courtesy Norwood Historical Society.)

a considerable number prepared to support regular services. By 1910, the congregation erected its first permanent home, a stucco and half-timber building of English design, located on a hillside at One Walpole Street, overlooking Washington Street at Guild Square. A rectory, also stucco, was built behind the church on Beacon Avenue. Unfortunately, the ledge rock embedded in the hillside prevented the full construction plans to be completed and, in 1962, a new facility was built on more spacious grounds on Chapel Street overlooking Disabled American Veterans Memorial Park.

When the Swedish Congregational Church disbanded in 1939, their building, farther down Chapel Street, became the home of the newly formed Norwood Church of the Nazarene. This church was subsequently incorporated in 1943 and, in 1967, acquired facilities on Route 1-A in Walpole. The more spacious Walpole structure enabled the membership to complement their regular religious services with youth groups, an adult fellowship, and a missionary society.

Meanwhile, the First Congregational Church of Norwood, the community's oldest established church, was itself undergoing a transformation. In 1884, the parish had moved into its fourth meeting place, a wooden shingle-style building on the northwest corner of Winter and Walpole Street and, in 1895, the parish formally assumed the name First Congregational Church. In subsequent decades, this building was enlarged, a board of trustees was created, and the church became affiliated with the United Church of Christ. In 1961, the congregation moved across Winter Street into its current brick, neo-Federal complex designed by architect Arland A. Dirlam.

Lastly, in 1966, the Temple Shaare Tefilah dedicated a new synagogue on Nichols Street, in the Westover area, to accommodate its growing congregation. While the first Jewish family arrived in Norwood in 1899, it was not until 1908 that a group of 17 families organized the Norwood Hebrew Congregation and were granted a charter. Services were held on high holidays in local halls such as Conger Hall, Odd Fellows' Hall, and the Elks' Building. In 1924, the congregation built the first Temple Shaare Tefilah on Washington Street opposite the Norwood Press facility. This served their needs for more than 40 years until the gracefully designed Nichols Street synagogue was erected.

For years, the Temple's congregation was led by familiar Norwood names such as the Cooper, Danovitch, Cushing, and Orent families. One of the Temple's longtime officers, Louis Orent, also became a prominent and generous community leader. Louis and Herman Orent established the original Orent Brothers store on Guild Street in 1912. The business moved to larger quarters in the Odd Fellows Building in 1927 and remained there until 1963 when a 10,000-square-foot store was built opposite the town common. As Orent's became a Norwood fixture, Louis Orent became active in community affairs. He was a member of the Greater Boston Salvation Army Advisory Board, an

The parsonage and fourth meetinghouse of the First Congregational Church was located on the corner of Winter and Walpole Streets until 1961. A professional building now stands at this site. (Courtesy Norwood Historical Society.)

honorary life trustee of Norwood Hospital, and a director of the Norwood Co-operative Bank. In 1933, he spearheaded the founding of the United Fund, then called the Community Chest, to sponsor community fundraising, and later became president of the Norwood Rotary Club and the Norwood Chamber of Commerce. When Orent's closed and the family retired out of state, it was a loss keenly felt by the entire town.

The decades between 1930 and 1970, then, were ones of remarkable change. The major industries that had been the life's blood of the town disappeared and were replaced by numerous research, development, and light manufacturing enterprises. Highways heralded a new age of transportation and mobility, and the words "commute" and "suburb" entered common usage. Residentially, individual construction of homes gave way to developments built en masse, apartment complexes, and category-housing such as elderly, veterans, and handicapped. The town struggled to maintain and even enhance municipal services with school, police/fire, and post office construction. Still, the core of the community remained somewhat unchanged as religious institutions, civic associations, and recreational facilities continued to provide a means for incoming residents to get to know new neighbors, who would eventually become friends.

The Temple Shaare Tefilah on Nichols Street was dedicated in 1966. It replaced the first Norwood temple, which stood on Washington Street near the junction of Chapel Street. (Courtesy Bryant F. Tolles.)

7. Music, Sports, and Recreation

Most graduates of Norwood High School can recall the school song, "Norwood," and its stirring words of loyalty to the "school on the hill." Many do not realize, however, that the hill referred to in the lyric is not the site of the present-day building, for the words and melody were written by John F. Wheelock in 1913, more than a decade before the high school on Nichols Street was constructed. The song itself actually refers to the town's first high school, later known as the Beacon School, located at the corner of Beacon and Bullard, on the hill behind the Morrill Memorial Library. The area surrounding the school building was known as Christian Hill, one of Norwood's first neighborhoods. Extending to the west of the town center, roughly between Vernon and Winter Streets, Christian Hill was home to the families of the town's businessmen, bankers, and professionals. While not as sublime as the mansions built by the industrialists, most of the homes on Christian Hill were sturdy and comfortable, with well-kept lawns and gardens. Many inhabitants were the descendants of the original Tiot settlers and had been in the community for generations, making the steady climb to success and respectability. Most were members of the First Congregational Church, the Universalist Church, or the First Baptist Church and the neighborhood was a close one.

Although some immigrants believed that these more established families looked down on them, and one resident of Christian Hill agreed that "some on the hill might have been a bit snobbish," their devotion to the town and its heritage cannot be questioned. It was, in large part, through this neighborhood's sense of civic-mindedness and community spirit that Norwood was born and prospered. It was also due to this group that music, sports, and other recreational activities became characteristic of the town, providing a sense of unity and shared entertainment to its diverse populations.

Nearly from its inception, Tiot reverberated with the sound of music for, in 1763, the Congregational community of the South or Second Parish formed a choir "to lead in singing the Psalms." It was a precedent-setting decision and the tradition of ecclesiastical music has carried forward to this very day via church choirs and musical presentations. About 100 years later, during the Civil War,

127

Norwood's first High School, later an elementary school called the Beacon School, was the "school on the hill" written of in the lyrics of the Norwood High school song. (Courtesy Hansen and Donahue Collection.)

some South Dedham residents became members of the Regimental Band of the 18th Massachusetts Volunteers. Upon their return to the town, in 1866, they organized the South Dedham Music Association under the leadership of William Fairbanks. In 1868, they changed their name to the South Dedham Union Cornet Band, but just in time for the incorporation of the town in 1872, the band became the Norwood Brass Band. Reorganized by local music teacher Bernard Colburn shortly thereafter, the band participated in area parades and concerts, was active in Civil War memorials, and presented summer concerts at the town's original bandstand, erected in 1903 at Aaron Guild Park. The Norwood Brass Band, eventually known as the Norwood Musicians Union Band, continued to be a mainstay in local musical events and parades throughout the twentieth century, disbanding in the 1990s after more than a century of distinguished service.

Alternating with the brass band on the Guild Square bandstand was the much-revered marching and concert band of the American Legion Norwood Post No. 70. Organized in the late 1920s, the unit competed and participated in American Legion conventions, winning the Massachusetts State Championship eight times between 1931 and 1941. Known as the Norwood Legionnaires, they too participated in regional parades for decades, along with the Norwood Junior Legion Band, formed in later years. Association bands were also a popular diversion with the Finnish Hall's Savel and the Norwood Press Band becoming two of the local favorites.

The Norwood Brass Band, founded shortly after the Civil War, became a favorite among townspeople. Here the band is posed in front of Norwood's first bandstand, located at the park near Guild Street. (Courtesy Norwood Historical Society.)

The American Legion Norwood Post No. 70 Band is pictured here during its reign as Massachusetts State Champion. The Legionnaires were the pride of Norwood for decades. (Courtesy American Legion Norwood Post No. 70.)

Other units familiar to Norwood were a succession of church drum corps, initiated, once again, by the First Congregational Church. Formed at the turn of the century by the Reverend Arthur Howe Pingree, who also organized one of the first Boy Scout troops in the United States, the Boys' Brigade often used the Civic grounds for drill practice. Pingree is also remembered for running a summer camp for children on the Annisquam River in Gloucester, where he tragically drowned in 1915 while trying to rescue two young girls caught in the water's current. He was posthumously awarded the Carnegie Medal for Heroism.

In the 1930s, another charismatic clergyman, Reverend Robert McAleer, organized a fife, drum, and bugle corps for boys at St. Catherine of Siena School. It was not the first attempt by the church to enter the music scene. In the early 1920s, Reverend Francis Phelan, one of the church's curates, had formed a drum corps. Disbanded due to lack of interest, the unit was continued by some former members as the Norwood Drum Corps and appeared in parades into the 1930s. When McAleer organized his school corps, the Norwood Drum Corps members provided much needed support and enthusiasm. This time, St. Catherine's group was a success from the start and McAleer quickly invited the school's girls to participate as well. These two units, proudly wearing the St. Catherine's name and colors, participated in parades and competitions throughout eastern Massachusetts, capturing the "Cardinal's Cup" in annual diocesan competitions. In 1940,

The Norwood Press Band, seen here on July 4, 1907, was made up primarily of employees of C.B. Fleming and Company, the bindery department of the Norwood Press. (Courtesy Norwood Historical Society.)

The Boys' Brigade, organized by Reverend Arthur H. Pingree of the First Congregational Church in the early 1900s, was the town's first boys marching drum and bugle corps. (Courtesy Norwood Historical Society.)

following the untimely death of Father McAleer, Reverend Christopher Griffin, another personable young curate, guided the units. Under his direction, the most experienced members were organized into two successful senior corps, one of which, the Senior Boys, was invited to escort the grand marshal of the New York City St. Patrick's Day Parade. They held this honor from 1942 through 1950.

When participation in the parochial school–sponsored units diminished in the post-war 1950s, St. Catherine's Drum and Bugle Corps was discontinued, but some members carried their musical interest into other venues. The veterans of St. Catherine's Girls Corps became the nucleus of the Norwood Debonnaires. Sponsored by the American Legion Norwood Post No. 70 and the Norwood Lodge of Elks, the "Debs" won honors consistently in the Mayflower Circuit of competition and were World Open All Girl Champs for four consecutive years in the early 1970s. They even performed at the then newly opened Walt Disney World in Florida. Known for their colorful uniforms and intricate marching maneuvers, this outstanding group brought much enjoyment and pride to the town before interest in the corps waned.

The fifers and drummers of St. Catherine's Senior Boys reorganized as well, but set out in a new direction. Discarding the big band sound and colorful costumes of their drum and bugle days, the group dressed in sleeveless waistcoats, leggings, and tri-cornered hats and marched to the slower cadence of the eighteenth century. Known as the Colonial Boys, they built up an extensive repertoire of Irish music as well, enabling them to capitalize on the popularity of that ethnic sound. The group has traveled to such places as South Boston, New York City, Hawaii, and Dublin and Galway, Ireland to perform in St. Patrick's Day parades. Celebrating their 50th anniversary in 2003, the group remains a crowd favorite.

Melodies of a different sort also wafted through the air as Norwood-based orchestras and combos were widely supported by local audiences. The music of groups led by Jim Slavin, "Wits" Phalen, and Charlie Drummey enlivened many nights at the Civic and other social halls, as did Lester Lee's "Tin Whistle and Orchestra" and Wally Dauksevitch and his "Beltones."

Norwood's school system has also provided the town with a wide range of musical groups. First led by music education director Jean Dethier in the 1930s and 1940s, the high school bands not only performed at athletic events but joined in the town's parades. Band director George Farnham, who also encouraged music with his Farnham's Music Store, located in the Hawkins Block on Washington Street, headed the school department's music program until the arrival of Paul Alberta in 1963. Arriving at a time when public school music programs were just beginning to gain the recognition and funding they deserved, Alberta developed Norwood's department into a system-wide, broad-based program that includes marching, symphony, and concert bands, a jazz ensemble, concert choral, madrigal singers, and jazz choir.

In the past 39 years, Alberta's students have earned an impressive collection of championships and awards. The Norwood Mustang Marching Band has won top honors at the Massachusetts Instrumental Conductors Association many times and has won medals at the International Music Festival in Bermuda. Between 1975 and 1983, they performed at New England Patriot home football games and have won first place in the All-American Music Festival Parade Competition. The Norwood High School Jazz Ensemble has an equally enviable record, having been awarded a Southeastern Massachusetts District 1-A rating for decades and the International Association of Jazz Educators Southeast District gold medal for 20 consecutive years, as well as gold and silver medals in international competitions. The small Jazz Combo also has won numerous state, regional, and national awards. The High School Symphony and Concert Bands toured nine European countries in 1972 while amassing their own top ratings and medals. In addition, the town's vocalists have emerged as a powerful force in various state and national competitions. Both the Madrigal Singers and the Jazz Choir have won first place at Orlando's All-American Music Festival and the Madrigal Singers have performed at the Kennedy Center for the Performing Arts in Washington, D.C. Today, the school's music program has several full-time instructors and enthusiasm among students only seems to increase.

Perhaps as proof that musical performance has become a life-long endeavor in Norwood, three years ago a Norwood Community Concert Band was organized. Made up of dedicated volunteers, the band performs at the very popular Concerts on the Common, held during the summer months at the Walter J. Dempsey Memorial Bandstand, erected in 1993. Reviving a tradition that had ended when Norwood's original bandstand was torn down in 1957, these concerts serenade enthusiastic crowds weekly. Norwood has also sponsored a popular Summerfest series of concerts for the past 23 years. These events, which feature a wide range of musical styles, are held on the Municipal Building lawn. Another community musical highlight is the ongoing series of carillon concerts. Refurbished in the 1980s, the carillon bells, located in the Municipal Building tower, are played by musicians throughout the year. When the wind is right, the sounds of this magnificent instrument can be heard for miles.

Norwood is very fortunate in that it has a proud heritage not only in music, but in sports. And, like the community and school musical organizations, the town's storied athletic past includes clubs, associations, and individual achievements as well as school league play.

To begin with, organized baseball was played in Tiot at least three years before Norwood's incorporation, when West Dedham, Walpole, and South Dedham engaged in competition. Ignored by most as "just noisy boys' games played after school," according to John Kiley Sr., Norwood's first professional baseball player, the sport gained little respect or interest until the mid-1870s. It was then that Tyler Thayer, a local building contractor, formed a team and practiced right in the village center. This got the attention of local merchants, who eventually purchased uniforms for the team. Kiley himself went on to play briefly with the Washington Nationals and the Lynn, Massachusetts team in the old New England League, but his parents' disapproval ended his promising career and he returned to Norwood to work in the car shops. Support for the sport continued to grow, however, and, by the turn of the century, the town-wide Junior Athletic League, founded by Reverend Arthur Pingree, was extremely popular among Norwood's young ballplayers. George Willett provided the equipment and games were played at Prospect Park, located between Vernon and Cottage Streets on Christian Hill, Morrill's Field in South Norwood, and Casey Field in Cork City.

These 1905 Junior Athletic League of Norwood champs include, from left to right, (front row) Johnny Schaeffer, Fred Peterson, Mel Smith, George Buckman, Earl Fenton, and Steve Hunt; (back row) Frank Schuster, Freeman Chase, George Mitchell, and Norman Schackley.

133

For older enthusiasts, several business establishments sponsored employee baseball teams that entertained local audiences as well. Norwood Press owner James Berwick saw the potential of an undeveloped piece of land with natural hills situated between Chapel Street and Walnut Avenue. In 1907, he and his partners converted the site into a clubhouse and beautiful park with a baseball diamond, running track, and spectator stands. The Norwood Press Club itself housed a meeting hall, library, bowling alleys, and pool tables. The club was comprised chiefly of employees of the press although eventually other Norwood residents could also join. Purchased by the Norwood Lodge of Elks in 1923, the grounds and fields, site of many hard-fought contests, were also utilized for carnivals, band concerts, and, in winter, sledding and ice skating.

As World War I loomed, Norwood produced a particularly fine athlete, Marty Callaghan, who, after graduating from Norwood High in 1916, went on to play 4 years of major league baseball and 11 minor league seasons with the Chicago Cubs and Cincinnati Reds in the National League. Callaghan was such a local hero that a Marty Callaghan Day was held with a fine turnout of both adults and aspiring young ballplayers. The Norwood Brass Band provided the musical entertainment. Even Callaghan's popularity was surpassed in the 1920s, however, by John Dixon, the 6-foot, 4-inch multi-talented giant who excelled in baseball, football, and basketball and became a local legend. Considered by many to be Norwood's greatest athlete, Dixon was the captain of the undefeated 1926

The c. 1909 Norwood Press baseball team included, from left to right, (front row) Allie Moulton, John Schaeffer, and Maughty Ahearn; (middle row) Obbie Keddy, Peter Schuster, Tom McCready, and Jim Pitchell; (back row) Bert Sparrow, Tap Geary, Bing Callahan, Ike Hawkins, Mike O'Leary, and manager Cephus Jackman.

Marty Callaghan Day included speeches, music by the Norwood Brass Band, and much frivolity among the young fans of Norwood's successful Chicago Cub. Callaghan can be seen in the center in his Cub uniform. (Courtesy Helen Abdallah Donohue.)

state championship football squad and the star of the high school's 1927 state championship baseball team. He went on to attain All-American status at Boston College, played for a time in semi-professional circles, and became a physical education instructor at Norwood Junior High.

The son of Lithuanian parents, Dixon and his career also gave rise to a certain amount of ethnic pride in South Norwood's immigrant community where athletics were seen as a means to assimilation. In 1923, the Knights of Lithuania organized a girls' sports program and, beginning in 1926, they supported the remarkable efforts of John Jasionis who, in his initial competition, won first prize as New England Schoolboy Diving Champion and, a year later, placed second in a national competition. On the other side of town, immigrants in Dublin and Cork City cheered on the Norwood Gaelic Football Club. The local squad competed against teams from Boston and the surrounding towns in front of an enthusiastic crowd. Meanwhile, in the Swedeville neighborhood, track and field was the favorite sport of the Finns. They competed within a regional Finnish circuit, developing a sports field at the site of their picnic grounds off Fisher Street in Walpole.

Two other sports, boxing and Roman-Greco wrestling, also gained a following within ethnic enclaves. Matches were held at various locations, including the South End Social Club and Lithuanian Hall. A Norwood Finn by the name of

Members of the Norwood Gaelic Football Club of 1915 include, from left to right, (front row) John Murphy, Mike Flaherty, Martin Lydon, and Patrick Lennon; (second row) Denny Kelliher, John Cotter, Andy Hazlett, William White, Jim Hazlett, Martin Costello, and Mike McDonough; (third row) assistant manager Danny Cullinane, John Collins, manager Tom Griffin, John Foley, and trainer Tommy Curtin; (fourth row) Denny Ryan, Pat Welby, Pat Hessian.

Maki became a wrestling lightweight champion, and John Dixon, who tried his hand successfully at boxing, once held his own in the ring against heavyweight contender Jim Maloney.

From its inception, the Norwood Civic Association offered a multitude of athletic programs in the gymnasium, on the playing fields, and on the tennis courts. For a time, the Civic also reopened the Turnhall on Wilson Street, calling it Winslow Hall. Sensing that the Germantown neighborhood was too far removed to participate in sports at the Civic itself, the organization utilized the former social center for, among other things, scout meetings, women's gymnastic classes, and boys' basketball.

Bowling and billiards, two other pastimes that were promoted at the Civic, caught on in all parts of town. There were alleys at the Civic, the Norwood Press Club, the South Norwood Social Club, in the Talbot Building, around the corner on Day Street, and at Julius Balduf's on Wilson Street, among other locations. Whether these were dark, neighborhood alleys or modern establishments, the sport became a favorite and competition was fierce. At the turn of the century, the outstanding bowling team in Norwood joined the regional New Century

League. By the 1940s, there were four well-known bowling alleys, the Cloverleaf, Roll-Land, the Sport Center, and Day Street, and the town had become a candlepin stronghold with dozens of leagues and teams. One of these establishments, the Norwood Sport Center on East Cottage Street, remains in business to this day. Nearly all social organizations from the Norwood Press Club to the Masons to the South End Social Club to the Civic had their own billiard and pool rooms. The sports were also played in the Talbot Building, at Karki's on Savin Avenue, and on Dean Street. The sport's popularity was so vast that during the influenza epidemic of 1918, billiard parlors and pool rooms were the last public gathering places to be closed.

Football as Americans play it was introduced to Norwood by the Ambrose brothers. Until their arrival in 1895, football was a rough and tumble form of rugby played on the Everett School yard by pick-up teams. But, by 1896, the Ambrose brothers had put together a team and used the street in front of their *Norwood Messenger* office as a playing field. Eventually, the town embraced the game and it became a high school sport, but it was not until the Benny Murray era that football really took hold.

Whenever sports in Norwood are discussed, the name of H. Bennett "Benny" Murray comes up. A three-sport coach at Norwood High School from 1922 until 1946, when he retired because of ill health, Murray amassed a record that would go unmatched. He inspired his players and they, in turn, attracted the town's attention with their competitive spirit. Eventually, the football field behind the

This 1917 Winslow Hall basketball team, sponsored by the Civic Association and featured in The Civic Herald, *included, from left to right, (front row) Albert "Rabbit" Blasenak, Frank Verderber, and Herbert Readel; (back row) Coach G.R. Hoadley, John "Mutt" Eppich, Ernest Knous, and Howard Ortla.*

high school was named in Murray's honor. It was a fitting tribute since football was Murray's first love and, in 25 years as a football coach, he directed the team to 20 winning seasons. Arguably the greatest football team ever to play at Norwood High emerged almost 35 years after Murray's departure, however. The Norwood High School 1980 squad won the Bay State League crown and became the Division I Super Bowl Champions. This team was ranked number one in the Northeast and number eight in the country. Twenty years later, the Mustangs made back-to-back Super Bowl appearances in 2000 and 2001, returning victorious in 2000.

Benny Murray was also a successful baseball coach. His teams participated in the schoolboy tournaments, then held at Fenway Park or Braves Field, six out of seven years between 1937 and 1943, capturing the state championship in the latter year. During that era, perhaps the town's best athlete was Ray Martin, the star of the 1942 Norwood Junior American Legion team that captured the state title and the 1943 state championship baseball team at Norwood High. Martin went on to pitch for the Boston Braves during the late 1940s, although his career was interrupted by military service. Martin was also an all-scholastic football player, competing on Murray's undefeated 1942 squad, and was a defenseman on Norwood's first ever hockey team. At that time, ice hockey was primarily an outdoor sport. There were no rinks that could be reserved in advance, so players

Believed by many to be the best baseball team in Norwood history, the 1942 Junior American Legion State Champs, seen here at Braves Field, included, from left to right, (front row) Pete Carchedi, John Drost, Francis Brennan, Fran Harrington, Charley Parker, Joe McDonough, and mascot Jim Donlan; (back row) Eddie Mulkern, Bob Stanton, Butch Tranavitch, Frank Miloszewski, Ray Martin, Kenny Berkland, Ken McDonald, Stanley Barylak, Eddie Praino, and Coach John Dixon. (Courtesy Ray Martin.)

and parents cleared whatever ice surface they could find. The Norwood team practiced at Pettee's Pond and Martin recalled that Norwood's initial game against Watertown at the Boston Arena was "the first time we ever played inside the boards and on artificial ice." Eventually, ice time was obtained at the Skating Club in Brighton and the Tabor Rink in Needham and league games continued to be played at the Boston Arena for decades. In 1964, Walpole's Four Seasons Arena opened up, providing an opportunity to practice and compete closer to home.

Another Norwood athlete who excelled in both baseball and hockey was Richie Hebner. A 1966 graduate of Norwood High, Hebner was offered a contract by the Boston Bruins and was the number one draft choice of the Pittsburgh Pirates. Taking the baseball offer, he was in the majors three years later. After an 18-year major league career, Hebner went on to coach for various teams, including the Boston Red Sox. In this era, two other Norwood greats made the big leagues, both as pitchers: Skip Lockwood, a Norwood Little League and Babe Ruth star, who went on to Catholic Memorial where he was considered one of the greatest athletes in that school's history, and Bill Travers, a lanky lefthander whose career with the Milwaukee Brewers was cut short by injury. In 1976, Norwood baseball fans organized a gala celebration for their three major league stars. First, there was a parade through town with Lockwood, Hebner, and Travers riding in an open convertible, escorted by the town's Little League players and serenaded by the Norwood High School Band and the Debonnaires. The next night they were guests of honor at a sold-out banquet where "Jumping" Joe Dugan, who played pro ball during the Babe Ruth–Lou Gehrig era, commented that he'd never known of any town that had three major league ballplayers at the same time "and that includes New York City, where there are seven million people."

The golden era of hockey in Norwood, according to Frank Wall, a devoted fan and local sportswriter who followed athletics in town religiously until his death in 1991, began in the 1960s under coach Don Wheeler. During his reign, the team traveled to the state finals four times, culminating in the 1972 victory that finally brought the state championship to Norwood. After a rebuilding decade, the team rebounded in the 1990s, and by the 2000–2001 season, had four successive Herget Division championships and two Bay State League crowns to their credit.

The tradition of Benny Murray's third sport, basketball, continues to this day as well. After decades of hard work and accomplishment, it was the 1983–1984 Norwood High squad that brought home the town's first Bay State League Championship. Four years later, the team had its best record ever in Norwood history and, by the turn of the century, was a perennial tournament participant. In Murray's time, of course, basketball was a low scoring game because there was a jump ball at center court after each basket, but times have changed.

Still, the most dramatic changes have occurred, understandably, in the realm of women's sports. From the town's inception until 1940, basketball and tennis were the only sports available to high school girls. By the 1960s, softball, gymnastics, field hockey, and swimming had been added. Today, of course, the girls athletic program contains opportunities, including cross country, soccer, volleyball, indoor track, ice hockey, and cheerleading. The past decade has been the most successful ever for girls' competition. Cross country teams garnered five consecutive Herget Division titles in the 1990s and the basketball team captured Bay State League crowns in 1993 and 1994. In the late 1990s, the basketball teams were aided by league standouts Alison and Andrea Dixon, granddaughters of legend John Dixon.

Despite all the successes of school-sponsored athletic programs, however, it is the local spots, places such as "Froggy's Pond," "Hartshorn's Swale," and the "Clay Pit," that longtime residents remember best. Ice skating was a favorite pastime at Dunn's Pond, where the combined police and fire station was erected in the 1960s, at "the Hollow" in South Norwood, and at today's Elks Park. Bonfires, sledding, pick-up games, fishing, swimming at New Pond, and canoeing on Ellis Pond are fondly recalled whenever folks are asked to reminisce.

Recreational organizations emerged as well. The Norwood Tennis Club was formed in 1900 to encourage lawn tennis, and the club held tournaments on grounds that were later to become civic association property. The Tiot Tennis Club, organized in 1903, built courts at the corner of Lenox and Cross Streets. At about the same time, the Norwood Athletic Club was founded. Headquartered at Village Hall, the club organized teams in a number of sports, held dances, and offered dramatic entertainment. A few years later, the Norwood Lodge of the Benevolent and Protective Order of Elks was organized. Meetings were held at

The 1902 Norwood High girls basketball team is pictured here. At the time, only basketball and tennis were available to high school girls. (Courtesy Norwood Historical Society.)

140

Skating at Dunn's Pond, now the site of Norwood's combined police and fire station, was a popular winter pastime for earlier generations.

Odd Fellows' Hall until 1923 when the group acquired the former Norwood Press Club and grounds. The Elks remodeled the old Press Club in the early 1960s and continue to be active within the community today. Still, for those with long memories, the Civic, with its tennis courts, ball fields, and swimming pool, remains the hands-down favorite.

The Civic encouraged non-athletic competitions as well. In 1917, for example, they sponsored a Girls Canning Club in conjunction with the Amherst Agricultural College. Seventy-four girls between the ages of 10 and 18 each canned at least 24 quarts of fruit and vegetables throughout the summer months. At the end of the season, an exhibit was held at the Civic and, although every girl was given some recognition in the competition, first place was awarded to Emily Hallowell, a 15-year-old, who had canned 250 quarts of fruits and vegetables. There was a serious purpose to the contest, however, as there was to the Civic-sponsored Gardeners Club, held that same year, which attracted about 300 schoolchildren. According to the *Civic Herald*, the crops and canned goods "helped feed ourselves, our soldiers, and our allies." For the remainder of World War I and thereafter, these kinds of activities served to bring the community together and reinforce public-spiritedness.

Yet another pastime of the twentieth century arrived with the invention of motion pictures. Available records indicate that the first motion pictures in Norwood were shown in one of the stores in the Fisher Block in 1907. This venture failed, as did showings held later in Village Hall, and in a tent set up on the corner of Cottage and Washington Streets by the Metropolitan Theatre Company. Finally, in 1910, Charles Hubbard opened the Premier Theatre on Washington Street. Later known as the Guild Theatre because of its proximity to Guild Square, the building eventually found new life as a bank building and, today, a restaurant. In 1913, the New South Theatre opened in South Norwood, much to the pleasure of the families living in that neighborhood. The building was also used as a gathering place for local organizations and neighborhood meetings. These two concerns remained in competition until the Premier

Emily Hallowell was awarded first place in the Norwood Civic Association's Girls Canning Club competition in 1917. The exhibition took place at the Civic. (Courtesy Morrill Memorial Library.)

Theatre Company opened the Norwood Theatre on Central Street, with much fanfare, on August 31, 1927.

Designed by William G. Upham, the theatre was an adaptation of the Spanish Romanesque style of architecture, chosen to blend with the then planned Memorial Municipal Building. The interior featured a marble terrazzo lobby floor and walls of Caen stone with a Notre Dame marble dado. The ornate cornice and ceilings were of ornamental plaster covered by gold leaf and color, and wrought-iron chandeliers and bracket lights lit the auditorium. In addition to an orchestra pit large enough to accommodate a 20-piece orchestra, a cathedral pipe organ with attachments was also installed. It was the town's showplace for a number of years. When times changed, the theatre was adapted for use as a moviehouse and, as the Norwood Cinema, eventually had two screens. In the 1990s, the building was restored by the non-profit Fiddlehead Theatre Company and became the home of live performances once again.

Next to the Norwood Theatre, at 101 Central Street, Furlong's Candies opened in 1931, having relocated from Washington Street where they had been in business for two years under the name Cloverleaf Candies. Ice cream was added to the product line in 1932, using ice delivered from the Ellis Pond by the Norwood Ice Company, an electrically powered salt and ice machine, and an extremely rich recipe. Throughout the next two decades, fork-dipped chocolates and handmade ice cream made Furlong's a household name. By the 1950s, it had become a high school gathering spot, especially after weekend athletic contests

The Norwood Theatre opened on August 31, 1927. Situated across from the town square, the building was designed by William Upham to blend with the planned Municipal Building. (Courtesy Hansen and Donahue Collection.)

when the small shop and adjoining sidewalk would fill with teens. In 1960, the family purchased La Rose Candies on Providence Highway, painted the building red, and named it Furlong's Cottage Candies. Six years later, the Central Street store was closed and in 1980, the Furlongs sold the business and retired to New Hampshire.

Other popular mid-century "hang-outs" were also located on Providence Highway as the automobile age ended the need for successful enterprises to be situated in the town's central business district. The memory of Neponset Valley Farm's Ice Cream stand, with its grazing cows and modern dairy facilities in the background, is a pleasant one for many families. An outgrowth of the Fisher Dairy, it stood on the southbound side of Route 1 until it was torn down for an apartment development and commercial ventures in the 1970s. Another favorite among area residents was Art Johnson's, a small Route 1 eatery known for having the best fried clams in town. A noted teen attraction, Art Johnson's was also the starting point for many an illegal drag race down the highway.

For those individuals who wanted to watch drag racing and other automobile-related sports, the Norwood Arena was the place to be. Situated on the northbound side of Providence Highway, on what had previously been the site of the town's sewer filtration beds, the property consisted of more than 70 acres. The Norwood Arena itself included a banked, quarter-mile racing oval, stands, and clubhouse. Built originally for Midget racers, the course was also used for Sportsmen, Modified, and NASCAR competitions, as well as demolition

Furlong's on Central Street near the Norwood Theatre, known for its fork-dipped chocolates and handmade ice cream, was a favorite spot for teenagers in the 1950s and early 1960s. (Courtesy Thomas Furlong.)

derbies. For a number of years, Johnny Most, famous for his Boston Celtics radio broadcasts, was the announcer. Eventually, arena management constructed a 1/8-mile drag strip to boost attendance. Races at the Norwood Arena drew avid fans for nearly 25 years, despite neighborhood complaints of disruption and noise. By the early 1970s, noise pollution laws, a fire in the clubhouse, and community disapproval combined to sound the death knell of the enterprise. The controversial drag strip was liquidated in 1971 with its spectator stands, timing tower, guard rail, and light poles all sold at auction. After multiple court actions and seemingly endless zoning and purchasing delays, the remainder of the vacant property was sold in 1976. By the early 1980s, known as Park Place, with streets with prestigious sounding names like Carnegie Row, Vanderbilt Avenue, and Morgan Drive, the site was zoned for limited manufacturing and some commercial development. It currently houses various business interests.

Not far from Norwood Arena, Roll-Land opened on Thanksgiving Day 1938 and became a regional draw of a different sort. The brainchild of Charles, Peter, and John Santoro, Roll-Land offered roller-skating, bowling, and, for a time, miniature golf. Following World War II, its success became nearly phenomenal. Amateur productions, professional competitions, student lessons, and skating for just plain enjoyment all co-existed at Roll-Land. The complex attracted families, serious athletes, and couples, especially on Thursday night, which was dance night. With the advent of the Roller Skating Rink Operators Association of America, the sport enjoyed the prestige of nationwide publicity and popularity and special buses brought avid participants to the rink on Saturday nights. Skating festivals highlighted the work of student skaters of all ages and abilities and dance competitions always drew a large audience. Among serious roller-skating enthusiasts of both speed and figure skating, Roll-Land acquired an enviable reputation as its members represented the skating emporium proudly in local, state, and national competitions. After a fire totally destroyed the building in 1962, a new Roll-Land rose from the ashes and continued for several more decades. The business was closed in July of 2000.

With the demise of the Norwood Arena in the 1970s, the sale of the Civic property in the 1980s, and the closing of Roll-Land in 2000, the recreational landscape of Norwood changed dramatically. Still, the replacement of these familiar concerns by innovative business ventures, hospital expansion, and a fitness center respectively, was indicative of the much broader, cultural transformation taking place in America as the millennium approached. Once again, the town of Norwood would strive to position itself for success and stability in a shifting economic environment yet, at the same time, maintain a commitment to, and continuity with, its past.

Roll-Land, a Norwood landmark for over 60 years, had a national reputation among roller skating emporiums and attracted skating enthusiasts from all over New England. (Don McLean photo.)

145

8. Moving Forward, Looking Back

In 1972, the town of Norwood marked its 100th anniversary with a year-long celebration that included dozens of events. Ranging from contests, concerts, picnics, and road races to a lavish centennial banquet held at Roll-Land and a gala Fourth of July parade, festivities were planned for, and enjoyed by, young and old alike. The calendar of activities came to a close in November with three events that captured the spirit of the town and its residents. First, an interfaith religious service, held at the Junior High North, celebrated the ecumenical nature of the community's numerous religious congregations. Within a week, this unifying occasion was followed by the traditional Thanksgiving Day football game with Dedham High School, held at H. Bennett Murray Field. An annual contest, the rivalry took on added significance 100 years after Norwood's separation from its mother town. And, finally, at the centennial celebration's closing ceremony, a marker was unveiled on the town common with the following inscription:

> Town of Norwood, 1872–1972. Dedicated to all her citizens, those of the past whose imagination, diligence, and hard work laid the foundation for her early heritage, those of the present who today pay tribute on her 100th anniversary, and those of the future who will be called upon to maintain her tradition.

This latter charge was to be quite a challenge as the town once again braced to withstand the trials of three more decades of rapid change. Still, Norwood managed to do what it seems to do best: moving forward and adapting while, at the same time, looking back and honoring its past.

First of all, from 1972 through 2002, the industrial and commercial landscape of the town was altered once again as major enterprises such as Raytheon, Masoneilan, and Northrop departed from the community. Still, by the turn of the twenty-first century, business expansion was again flourishing. Analog Devices, Micron Corporation, and CertainTeed kept the town's manufacturing base thriving while the large distribution centers of Martignetti Companies

The days when the intersection of Washington Street and Railroad Avenue looked like this are long past. In this early twentieth-century view, Clark's Pharmacy in the Conger Block is on the right and the Norwood Laundry, then owned by Charles W. Fanning and Richard A. Mandeville, is on the left.

and United Parcel Service brought a new dimension of commerce into the community. Medical laboratories such as Imugen helped the town keep pace with the biomedical explosion and Putnam Investments, which took over the Forbes estate property in 2000, brought a piece of the global financial world to Norwood. Meanwhile, retail giants displaced numerous small commercial businesses. Neighborhood grocers such as Keating's and Farioli's Markets gave way to the A&P, Stop & Shop, and First National food chains, but, by the late 1980s, even larger "super stores" were cornering the market. The mantra of "bigger is better" ruled in the hardware trade as well, with family-run stores like Norwood Hardware and South End Hardware closing in the face of NHD and Ashmont. A short time later, these very same concerns were in jeopardy as HQ and Home Depot constructed competing warehouse-sized stores.

Commercial buildings in the downtown area stood empty as the once familiar Orent's, Parke Snow's, Gearty's Shoes, Andy's Jewelers, Woolworth's, and Grant's lost their clientele to shopping centers, plazas, and mammoth shopping malls, most conveniently located on the highway. The Guild, Balch, and Clark's pharmacies, to name a few, were also swallowed up by the likes of CVS, Osco, Brooks, and Walgreens. While residents mourned the loss of these local businesses and the personal service and simpler lifestyle they had come to symbolize, they were inevitably lured away by lower prices and huge inventories.

The largest and most successful businesses in Norwood became the automobile dealerships, as the proliferation of showrooms along Providence Highway led to the area being dubbed "the Automile" by the mid-1970s. There had, of course, been car dealerships prior to the development of the highway, but they, like other commercial ventures, were clustered in the downtown area. In

147

1917, C.A. Stuntzer opened the Norwood Buick Company at 649 Washington Street and, a short time later, relocated his showroom to Cottage Street. Within five years, Carl Johnson was selling Cadillacs at his Norwood Automobile Company, situated at the corner of Washington and Cottage Streets. It later became Norwood Cadillac and moved to Broadway in the 1930s and to Route 1 in 1971. Johnson himself was a well-respected businessman who was honored at a testimonial dinner only months before his death in 1978. By the 1930s and 1940s, Henry Hentschel's Walpole Street Garage, at the corner of Wilson Street, sold Studebakers, and small dealers such as Knox & Smith, who sold Dodge and Chrysler, Balboni's Central Motors, and Tony Sansone's DeSoto-Plymouth dealership, dotted the area.

After the construction of the Providence Highway was completed, Andrew Boch opened the first dealership on Route 1 in 1946. Today, the name of Ernie Boch is synonymous with the term Automile, a nickname Boch himself coined. Rambler, Oldsmobile, Toyota, Mitsubishi, Kia, and Honda are among the dealerships that have carried the Boch name. Other local dealers were quickly drawn to the roadway built for automobile travel, including many familiar names such as Jack Madden, John Mack, and Louis Stuntzner, son of the Norwood Buick Company founder. In 1958, the Norwood Automobile Dealers Association was organized to coordinate efforts among dealers to better serve the customers of Norwood and the surrounding towns. One longtime member of the association was Herb Anderson, president of the Volkswagen dealership. Anderson had previously operated the Vega Swedish Restaurant on Providence Highway for 27 years and was a one-term member of Norwood's Board of Selectmen. Today, the Automile, once a landscape of farms and fields, is a thriving, seemingly endless string of car sales, rentals, and service enterprises.

Residentially, the 1970s brought the first condominiums and condo-conversions to Norwood. This new method of ownership, whereby living space formerly considered rental apartment property, was sold as individual homes, contributed to an expanded tax base for the town. Although the tax rate itself decreased, the assessed valuation of property in Norwood increased nearly ten times between 1972 and 1993. Still, some residents warned of the potential hazards of speculators buying the relatively inexpensive condominiums as investments and renting them. Nearby Westwood even considered banning condominiums, fearing such complexes would become "the slums of tomorrow." Open space continued to disappear as apartment complexes, new and converted condominiums, and single-family subdivisions seemed to sprout up on every patch of grass. Sadly, several Victorian-era structures, including the Tilton mansion on Beech Street and the Cushing home on Highland Avenue, were moved or removed to make way for new construction.

The population reached its peak at about 32,000 shortly after Norwood's centennial year and has hovered around 28,000 during most of the last three decades. A significant decline in the number of school-age children led to the closing of the Winslow, Guild, Shattuck, and Willett elementary schools and the

Junior High North. These former school buildings were put to good use, however. The junior high building was leased to a number of concerns, the Shattuck was converted to senior citizen housing, and the Willett became the home of school administrative offices. The former West and Winslow Schools, which had each housed school administration for a number of years, and the Aaron Guild School on Washington Street, were sold and converted into medical office buildings as were several fine old homes in the Walpole and Washington Street area.

This latter usage made clear the importance to the town of the Norwood Hospital, not merely as a healthcare facility, but as an employer and the catalyst for development. Physicians, laboratories, and ancillary services associated with the hospital have contributed to the community through employment opportunities, tax revenues, and consumer patronage. In 1982, the Norwood Hospital formed the Neponset Valley Health System, a multi-institutional system designed to provide the most comprehensive package of services possible within the region. Other components of the NVHS included Southwood Community Hospital, formerly Pondville Hospital in Norfolk, Foxboro Area Health Center, Plainville Area Health Center, the NORCAP Center for Alcoholism, Norfolk-Bristol Home Health Services, and the Neponset Valley Foundation. In 1985, the hospital's Joseph J. Lorusso Building, which included a nuclear medicine diagnostic laboratory, a clinical laboratory addition, a ten-bed maximum care unit, and more in-patient floors, was completed. In 1997, the Norwood Hospital became part of the Caritas Christi Health Care System and an extensive renovation is currently underway. Despite dissatisfaction among some residents regarding the sale of the Recreation Department property for the hospital expansion of the 1980s, most are pleased that, under the ownership of the Caritas Christi network, the institution has made a significant turnaround and is once again on a firm financial footing. Today, the hospital's patient revenues

Erected on land that was formerly part of the Norwood Civic Association, the Joseph J. Lorusso Building increased the size and facilities of the Norwood Hospital in the 1980s. In 1997, Norwood Hospital became part of the Caritas Christi Hospital Network.

The Norwood Airport was founded in 1942 by a special town meeting. This aerial photo was taken 20 years later, in the mid-1960s. (Aerial Photos of New England photo.)

are up, both in- and out-patient numbers are on the rise, and the refurbished emergency room is the ninth busiest in the state.

Another distinctive enterprise of vital importance to the continued growth of the community is the Norwood Airport. The history of the airport actually begins, in part, just outside of Norwood, in 1932 when Wiggins Airways, one of a small number of general aviation concerns in the United States, began operations in an airport on Neponset Street in Canton, Massachusetts. The company sold aircraft parts and supplies, new and used planes, made repairs, and offered flight training. With the advent of World War II, Wiggins expanded its operations to other states and developed civilian training with government support in conjunction with area colleges and universities.

Meanwhile, in 1942, a Norwood town meeting approved the construction of the Norwood Airport on more than 400 acres of land in the northeastern section of town. This Fowl Meadows parcel had been deeded to the town by a group of local businessmen who had operated a small airfield there since the early 1930s. The airport was to be built at federal expense, maintained by the town, and kept available should any defense needs arise in the future. Military pilots received training at the new facility during World War II. Some residents may recall one particular mishap when a Navy pilot crashed on Chapel Street on August 7, 1944, causing a great deal of excitement, but no serious injuries.

Following the war, these two joint ventures came together when, in 1946, Wiggins moved its local operations from Canton to the new, larger Norwood site in time to capitalize on the increased interest in commercial and pleasure aviation. The firm established regular passenger, cargo, and mail routes and added a helicopter operation to its services. In addition, Wiggins continued to operate a flight school, offer charter services, maintain its parts and repair facilities, and engage in some light manufacturing. They were also one of the largest distributors of Piper aircraft in the country. Beginning in 1967, a 20-year lease authorized Wiggins to manage the airport under the supervision of the Norwood Airport Commission, and the entire Wiggins enterprise, including its offices, hangars, shops, parts store, and aircraft showroom, were housed at Norwood. It quickly became one of the busiest private fields in the New England region because of its location, approach lines, and facilities. Today, the airport encompasses several hundred acres, has two runways, and can accommodate single and multi-engine planes, jets, and helicopters. For a time after the departure of Wiggins, the airport was managed by the Boston Metropolitan Airport, Inc. but since June of 1999, control has rested with the Norwood Airport Commission who oversee a full-time airport manager, responsible for the day-to-day operation of the airfield.

Still a subject of controversy, particularly among its neighbors whenever expansion is discussed, the airport has become an economic asset to the community. In addition to recreational pilots, commercial companies use the airport for medical and organ donor flights, sightseeing tours, aerial photography, and flight training, among other activities. The airport has also become the temporary headquarters for the Norwood police and fire departments while their new facility is being constructed on Nahatan Street. The continuing commitment by Norwood officials and the support of citizens have enabled the Norwood airport to play an important role in both the local economy and the state transportation system.

Demographically, while the population of Norwood remains stable, the town continues to be ethnically diverse. According to the 2000 United States Census, Norwood is one of only three towns in the region whose percentage of foreign-born residents is at or higher than the state average. Almost half of these immigrants have arrived within the past decade and many have young families. This is reflected, in particular, by elementary school programs that highlight immigration to Norwood, multi-culturalism, and Asian studies. Today, children from more than 20 countries, including Albania, Korea, India, Japan, Uganda, Chile, and Brazil, attend the public schools.

South Norwood remains the most culturally diverse district in the community. Beginning in the late 1970s and early 1980s, the neighborhood attracted a large contingent of Portuguese families who, like other nationalities before them, organized a social association, the Norwood Portuguese Club. Unlike many earlier groups, however, the Portuguese quickly participated in town-wide events, becoming a favorite in the Fourth of July parade each year. Recently, the stability of the South Norwood neighborhood and rising real estate values have resulted in apartment complexes, such as Windsor Gardens and Norwest Woods, being the most affordable first stop for chain migrations from the Middle East, Russia, and India. Many Indian families worship at the Jain Center of Greater Boston, located in the Cedar Street building that was the former home of the Swedish Lutherans, and later, the Italian Christian Church. One of the oldest Eastern religions, Jainism encourages an individual approach to worship. Its main principles include non-violence, disdain for possessions, and a respect for all living things and perspectives. Established in 1973, the Jain Center of Greater Boston met periodically in rented halls at Harvard University and the Massachusetts Institute of Technology until it acquired the Cedar Street site in 1981. The temple's members note that they are the first Jain adherents to organize in the United States and, unlike any temple they are aware of in the world, the two sects of Jainism are united as one.

The continuing influx of immigrant populations is also reflected in the proliferation of ethnic markets and restaurants. Today, the town boasts of two Indian grocers, a Middle-Eastern market, and three Italian specialty stores. Ethnic restaurants have also played an important role in the revitalization of the commercial district which had languished throughout the 1980s and 1990s. Within the past few years, Norwood has become a popular dining attraction with more than a dozen eateries, coffee shops, and fine restaurants situated along Washington Street from Howard Street in the north to Mylod Street in the south.

The town continues to be responsive to the needs of its residents and services remain at a high level as town officials and citizen volunteers cooperatively work together, anticipating problems and seeking solutions. Municipal renovation and construction projects are ongoing, overseen by the town's volunteer Permanent Building Construction Committee. On a large scale, a $4-million renovation to the Morrill Memorial Library, paid for by a combination of state grant money, library trust funds, town appropriation, and private donations, was completed in 2001. By early 2003, the new police and fire station will be ready for occupancy. Meanwhile, several smaller restoration and maintenance projects at other town-owned facilities are underway.

Conservation and recycling programs are expanding; the town's electric light department is preparing to enter the cable business in an attempt to control costs; and the town meeting recently voted to explore the utilization of the Buckmaster Pond facility as an adjunct water supply. Spearheaded by longtime library trustee Eleanor H. Monahan, the Morrill Memorial Library began a literacy program in 1983 to provide free, one-on-one, confidential instruction to adults in basic reading and in English as a second language. Since that time, the program has become one of the largest in the state. Students come from varied backgrounds and range in age from teens to senior citizens. Their aspirations, too, vary from those who want to get a high school diploma, register to vote, or become a United States citizen to those who simply want to read a newspaper or a bedtime story to their children. Although a majority of students and tutors are from Norwood, this worthwhile program also serves many surrounding towns in southeastern Massachusetts.

Within the last few years, residents, neighbors, and town officials have united behind yet another joint venture, a restoration of the George H. Morse house located in South Norwood, near the junior high. Home to a direct descendant of the town's first permanent settler, Ezra Morse, the house was constructed in the mid-nineteenth century and was acquired by the town of Norwood around 1980. Since that time, the property has fallen into disrepair, but the restoration committee envisions meeting rooms, classroom space, and an area set aside for exhibits on Norwood history. According to one restoration committee member, the aim is "to preserve the past for the future."

In many respects, however, Norwood is a community that has always taken its heritage seriously and has cultivated its collective memory. It was 100 years ago, in 1902, that the Aaron Guild commemorative stone was placed on the library's lawn during an Old-Home Week celebration held under the auspices of the Norwood Business Association. A year later, a second stone monument was unveiled in Guild Square. In a grand ceremony that included guest speakers and a performance by the Norwood Brass Band, the Siege of Louisburg stone, as it is known, pays tribute to the nine men from South Dedham who participated in that military action during the French and Indian War.

Parks, playgrounds, and recreational facilities throughout the town have been named for respected groups and individuals. For example, Winslow Park, deeded to the town in 1898 by the Winslow family, is now Disabled American Veterans Memorial Park and the town common is officially the Veterans of Foreign Wars Square. The former Wilson Street playground, founded through the efforts of that Germantown neighborhood, is the James J. Gormley Playground, and Father Mac's, as it is popularly known, the field and pool at the head of Vernon Street, is named for Reverend Robert McAleer, the well-liked St. Catherine curate. The town's other outdoor pool, Hawes Pool in South Norwood, may be named for the brook that runs nearby, but the Nicholas Abdallah Auditorium at the Balch School is a tribute to the good works of the Abdallah family in general and "Nick" in particular. Likewise the dedication of the Walter J. Dempsey Memorial

The unveiling of the Siege of Louisburg commemorative stone was held on July 23, 1903 and included a blessing by clergy and musical selections from the Norwood Brass Band. (Courtesy Norwood Historical Society.)

Bandstand on the town square in 1993 is a lasting memorial to a well-respected local businessman and long-term selectman.

Those citizens who have sacrificed for the community and the country are embraced by Norwood, beginning with memorial corners, individual plaques in honor of those who lost their lives in time of war. Each plaque is erected, at the request of family members, near the veteran's Norwood residence. In addition, a monument erected "in memory of all Marines of Norfolk County who gave their lives for our country" by the Norfolk County Marine Corps League, now stands in Aaron Guild Park.

As has been noted, the town hall is officially the Norwood Memorial Municipal Building, constructed as a perpetual tribute to those who served in World War I. On the lawn of the building stands a captured World War I artillery piece and mount, presented by the American Legion Norwood Post No. 70 at the building's dedication ceremony on November 11, 1928. Inside the cathedral-like edifice, the Memorial Chapel is a stirring tribute to those who fought in all conflicts from the Colonial Wars to the present day. On Veterans' Day 2002, the town will dedicate four large wooden plaques, installed on the walls of Memorial Hall, as a permanent memorial to those who died in the service of the United States in World War I, World War II, Korea, Vietnam, and the Persian Gulf. Also this year, the airport, called variously the Norwood Airport, the Norwood Municipal Airport, and the Norwood Memorial Airport since its inception, will be dedicated to all veterans with the installation of a new flagpole and commemorative plaque.

An often overlooked memorial to Lithuanian veterans of World War II stands on the parish property of St. George Catholic Church in South Norwood. Erected

The Norwood Firefighters Memorial dedication ceremony was held on May 20, 2001. Since that time, "Big Jake," as he is affectionately known, has stood guard at Highland Cemetery on Winter Street. (Don McLean photo.)

At Highland Cemetery stand a cannon placed there by the George K. Bird GAR Post 169 in memory of South Dedham veterans of the Civil War and a memorial to the Unknown Dead of that same conflict. (Courtesy Hansen and Donahue Collection.)

in 1949, the monument consists of a foundation and pedestal of Westerly, Rhode Island granite topped by a striking marble statue of St. George commemorating the 152 members of the parish who served, and the seven parishioners who gave their lives, "for God and Country."

Across town, at the Highland Cemetery, in addition to the sacred land where veterans are interred, stand three military monuments: the Civil War cannon dedicated by the George K. Bird Grand Army of the Republic Post 169 in memory of South Dedham comrades who lost their lives in the War of the Rebellion; a memorial to the Unknown Dead of that same conflict, erected in 1905 by the GAR Women's Relief Corps; and a bronze relief tribute to World War I veterans, dedicated in 1921 by the American Legion Norwood Post No. 70 "in memory of their comrades who in the world war, on land and sea, fought valiantly, suffered, endured, gave all in service and gained through death, immortal life." Also at the Highland Cemetery can be found the Norwood Police Association Memorial honoring the departed members of the Norwood Police Association, unveiled in 1995, and "Big Jake," the Norwood Firefighters Memorial. The monument, friendship walk, and meditative benches were erected in 2001 and honor Norwood's firefighters of the past, present, and future.

This last monument was created by sculptor Robert Shure of Woburn, Massachusetts, who also designed the Municipal Building's memorial plaques to be dedicated in November 2002. Shure is best known in Norwood, however, for his creation of the "Protectors of the American Way" monument that stands on the town common at the corner of Washington and Nahatan Streets. This sincere tribute was made possible by longtime Norwood resident, businessman, and real estate developer Frank Simoni. A veteran of two wars, Simoni was impressed by the remarkable monuments he saw while visiting Europe. In 1988, he decided he wanted to memorialize, on a grand scale, "those who sacrificed their lives to protect freedom." The final product, three 9-foot figures—a father, mother, and child—represents the American family and is guarded on three sides by bronzed military personnel representing the nation's armed forces.

The Protectors of the American Way monument is not only a lasting tribute to Simoni's abiding commitment to the town, but is emblematic of the multi-generational loyalty that many families maintain for this community. From its initial days as Tiot, Norwood has inspired a special kind of affection among its residents. It is a remarkably stable place, where people are proud to say their parents and grandparents were born and raised. Although no one individual has dominated civic affairs as George Willett did, many public-spirited citizens have participated in the growth of the town and have passed their dedication on to siblings, sons, daughters, and grandchildren. They, in turn, have taken on the responsibility and joy of preserving a community they all love. From the days of Reverend Thomas Balch, clergyman, citizen, and soldier of the Colonial Wars, to John Kilkus, a 26-year-old Norwood-born Marine Corps staff sergeant who lost his life in the Persian Gulf, more than 4,400 townspeople have answered the call to military service. Meanwhile, countless others have been "Protectors of the American Way" at home. Through elective office, volunteer associations, community activism, and unacknowledged individual good works, they have collectively endeavored to sustain a hometown like no other. If the past is any indication, Norwood's future will be filled with obstacles and uncertainty, but its residents will be up to the challenge.

"The Price of Freedom is Eternal Vigilance," intones the Protectors of the American Way monument erected across from the Norwood Memorial Municipal Building on the Veterans of Foreign War Memorial Square. (Courtesy Hansen and Donahue Collection.)

BIBLIOGRAPHY

The Centennial Celebration of the First Universalist Church, Norwood, Massachusetts, October 22nd and 23rd, 1927. Norwood: n.p., 1927.

The Civic Herald. Norwood: Norwood Civic Association, miscellaneous issues, 1913–1918.

Commemorating the 75th Anniversary of Saint Catherine of Siena Church. Norwood: n.p., 1965.

Cook, Louis A., ed. *History of Norfolk County, Massachusetts, 1622–1918*. 2 vols. New York and Chicago: The S.J. Clarke Publishing Company, 1918.

Curtis, Verna Posever and Jane Van Nimmen (ed.). *F. Holland Day: Selected Texts and Bibliography*. Oxford, England: Clio Press, 1995.

Grove, John M. *Images of America: Norwood*. Charleston, SC: Arcadia Publishing, 1997.

Hanson, Robert B. *Dedham, Massachusetts, 1635–1890*. Dedham, MA: Dedham Historical Society, 1976.

History and Directory of Norwood, Massachusetts for 1890. Boston, MA: Brown Brothers, 1890.

List of Persons Twenty Years of Age and Upward in the Town of Norwood With Their Residence, Occupation, and Age. Boston, Dedham, and Norwood: Several publishers, 1893–2000. Published under various titles.

Lockridge, Kenneth A. *A New England Town: The First Hundred Years—Dedham, Massachusetts, 1636–1736*. New York: W.W. Norton and Company, Inc., 1970.

Lothrop's Norwood, Mass., Directory. Boston: Union Publishing Co., 1924, 1928, 1931, 1933, 1936, 1938, 1942.

Norwood, Massachusetts. Information Files, Morrill Memorial Library.

Norwood Messenger, comp. *Official Commemoration and Chronicle Issued in Honor of the 75th Anniversary of the Town of Norwood*. Norwood: Norwood Daily Messenger, 1947.

Norwood Messenger, comp. *Town of Norwood 90th Anniversary Edition*. Norwood: Norwood Messenger, 1962.

Norwood Messenger, comp. *Official Commemoration and Chronicle—100th Anniversary, Town of Norwood*. Norwood: Norwood Messenger, 1972.

Norwood 125, Celebrating 125 Years of Grandeur. Dedham: Daily Transcript, 1997.

Norwood, One of the Newest and Most Progressive Towns in Massachusetts. Norwood: Ambrose Bros., Printers, *c.* 1906.

Resident and Business Directory of Norwood and Walpole, Massachusetts. Boston: Union Publishing Co., Inc., 1911, 1913–1914, 1916, 1918.

Sample, John Jr. and R.A. Messervey. *Picturesque Norwood.* Norwood: n.p., 1885.

Souvenir Album of Norwood, Massachusetts. Norwood: Hunt's 5, 10, and 25 Cent Stores, 1909.

Tolles, Bryant F. Jr. *Norwood: The Centennial History of a Massachusetts Town.* Norwood: Norwood Printing Co., 1973.

Town of Dedham, 325th Anniversary; Dedham Transcript, 90th Anniversary. Dedham: Dedham Transcript, 1960.

Transcript Press, Inc. Celebrating a Century of Service, 1870–1970. Dedham: Transcript Press, Inc., 1970.

Westover: A New England Village of the Twentieth Century. Norwood: Plimpton Press, *c.* 1934.

Willett, George F. *Can Business Methods be Applied to the Conduct of Municipal Affairs?* Boston: n.p., 1915.

Wolkovich, William. *Lithuanians of Norwood, Massachusetts: A Social Portrait in a Multi-ethnic Town.* Norwood: n.p., 1988.

The aerial view of the Norwood Arena was taken in 1973 after the drag strip had been dismantled. The strip itself can still be seen on the left with the racing oval on the right. (Aerial Photos International Photo.)

INDEX